Police Co[...]

In Yorkshire and Lincolnshire

(Part Two)

By

James Marchbank

Copyright © 2022 James Marchbank

ISBN: 9798801163413

All rights reserved, including the right to reproduce this book, or portions thereof in any form. No part of this text may be reproduced, transmitted, downloaded, decompiled, reverse engineered, or stored, in any form or introduced into any information storage and retrieval system, in any form or by any means, whether electronic or mechanical without the express written permission of the author.

CHAPTER 1

THE GOOD THE BAD AND THE DODGY

In the centre of what I regard as my city is a large and imposing building. It is a three storey, stone-built structure erected in the mid nineteenth century. It was built as the showpiece of a railway company that saw the city and their trade about to expand rapidly. Local people were not enthused by the project to build the hotel. They regarded it as a folly that would remain empty.

By the time the building was finished, and the hotel was ready to open, the person who had commissioned the work was in disgrace. His fraudulent business deals had been exposed in dramatic style. The hotel itself has, however, traded with total honesty and it went on to flourish in the years between then and now. Queen Victoria and Albert, the Prince Consort, were resident there and effectively took the hotel over for several days. It ceased to be a railway hotel and became the Royal Hotel. However, the fraud of the original owner sets the scene for the story I am about to tell.

I have booked into the hotel and found it to be light and bright with all surfaces sparkling and shining. There is a Grand Piano in the foyer, and it has a feel of a luxurious past and days long gone. When I visited it was a short stay, occasioned by an imminent house move. We had sold one house and our furniture had gone into store while we completed the purchase of our new house. My son was only two at the time and as we entered the hotel through its large, arched doorway he said,

"The new house is very big Daddy!"

Our room did indeed feel homely, and an extended stay would have been welcome. However, I have digressed because the events I will tell you about took place several years before my stay. Indeed, you need to focus on the late nineteen eighties.

On the day in question, it was very quiet and staff in the hotel were taking their leisurely time to complete their tasks.

In the rear car park of the hotel there were a couple of smart private cars. There was also a shabby, white transit van. The van did not seem to belong there and two men in suits were in the process of taping off the area occupied by the van. This unusual activity was noted by a hotel maid and after a short time she dragged herself from her vantage point and rushed off to tell the duty manager what was happening.

Five minutes later she was discussing what she had seen with a porter. It was there that the duty manager found her.

"Have you finished Alice or is this an official break?" The manager asked.

"No Mr. Wood. I was looking for you."

"Well, you have found me Alice. What is it?"

"Well, do you know about men in the car park who are putting tape round a van?"

"No. I do not. We have no workmen in today. Can you go and ask them please?"

"Not really my job Mr. Wood. More a management job. Asking people what they're doing. But I will for you if you like?"

"Yes, please Alice."

The maid wandered off towards the rear of the hotel. She was quietly pleased that she was on a mission for the duty manager.

At the same moment as Alice was speaking to the duty manager a blue minibus was approaching the entrance to the hotels' car park. The driver was Sean Hennessey, he was wearing a short-sleeved shirt and his forearms were heavily tattooed. The six or seven passengers in the bus were all smartly dressed. They had an aura of affluence about them and probably represented most of the business sectors operating in the city. There was a relaxed atmosphere among the passengers as if they were on a social day out.

As the minibus swung into the car park the driver and the passengers simultaneously saw the suited men and the taped off van. The driver seemed shocked.

"Arseholes!" Hennessey exploded. "Fucking Hell, they're coppers!"

He turned the van round in the car park and roared off along the road he had arrived by.

Alice arrived in the car park just as the minibus left. The suited men were taking down the tape that they had earlier put there.

"What're you doing?" She asked the men.

"Fuck off you. We're coppers." Snarled the taller of the two men.

Alice was shocked by this. She did not expect that policemen would speak to her like that. At the same time, she formed an opinion that they were not really what they said they were. The shorter one did not look like he had shaved for a few days and the taller one had tattoos on his fingers. She decided to go and get Mr. Wood and hurried off to do that.

By the time Alice had found the duty manager the suited men had got into the van, and they also drove out of the car park. It was as if nothing had ever happened. Mr. Wood did not think that he needed to do anything, and things went back to normal.

Now I would probably not have heard what happened next if a friend did not work for one of the men in the minibus. She told me what he had told her, and her boss subsequently asked me for advice.

The minibus travelled about two miles from the hotel and pulled up in a street of derelict houses. There the passengers were keen to be on their way. The relaxed atmosphere of earlier was replaced by anxiety near on panic. They all saw their worlds about to fall down because they had been involved in a get rich quick scheme, a scheme that was very far from legal.

Hennessey was a businessman of sorts. He ran a rather dubious security company which supplied door staff to night clubs and night watchmen for businesses. Some of the staff employed were only recently returned from 'Her Majesties Pleasure'. He provided staff to two of the passengers in the minibus. All the passengers would not want to socialize with Hennessey, but they had been attracted by the scheme he had put to them.

Hennessey told them that he had come into possession of a large amount of Lysergic Acid (which was an essential component of the drug LSD). He told them he had it in liquid form, but it needed refining and impregnating into blotting paper. He had found a lab in Southport which would do the work. He had enough chemical to make three hundred thousand tabs which he could 'retail' at between two and ten pounds. He reckoned that he would clear half a million pounds, but he did not have the money to pay the Lab costs.

He asked the businessmen to buy stakes in units of five thousand pounds a time and they would be looking at recovering ten times their 'investment'. He promised the businessmen that he would show them the Lysergic Acid and one of them could accompany the drug to the Lab. The trip to the car park had come after his 'investors' had already put up their money. They were all outwardly honest people with a stake in the city and if the Police traced the drug to them or even to Sean Hennessey then their reputations could come crashing down.

The businessmen scattered to their homes and places of work. They were all scared that they had come close to being exposed as fringe criminals/dodgy businessmen. Their reputations would be in shreds. Yet as the days went by and there was no visit from the police and no contact from Hennessey their fear started to be replaced with anger at the loss of their money. One or two suspected that they had been duped and one in particular considered compounding his dodgy dealings by hiring criminals willing to give Hennessey a good beating.

Now, you will have grasped that I hold the business community of my city in very low esteem. Any get rich quick scheme appealed to a sector of them and some were willing to get involved however dodgy the deal might be. But fact is stranger than fiction and when Hennessey went back with another scheme most of the first group were sucked in again. This time there was a large quantity of heavy copper wire in a

Russian port on the Baltic. It was necessary to hire a large ship and simply load it up. The returns could be even better than with LSD. At least half chipped in and waited for the copper to arrive.

Of course, there was no copper and Hennessey had a story about Russian Mafia and the Russian Governments' anti-corruption drive. The purchase was being investigated by the authorities in Russia and there was a possibility that the British Government would look into the UK side of the deal. Hennessey assured them that he would take the fall for the entire group if an investigation took place.

The businessmen had been taken again and this time a higher level of anger was reached. My friends' boss was even willing to give evidence against Hennessey in a fraud trial. I explained to him that he and his associates were in effect conspiring to commit offences, but he was adamant that the Russian purchase was merely a commercial contract, certainly if the copper had actually existed. I handed the job over to the CID and a statement was taken and a deal agreed for those who gave evidence.

Hennessey was arrested and remanded in custody. Things looked like working out as the businessmen sought revenge. Sadly, their nature caused the stack of cards to fall down. On a train, travelling to the Crown Court trial, two of them broke out a bottle of champagne in their First-Class compartment. As they consumed the alcohol the men became quite vociferous, congratulating themselves on their cleverness. However, they should have assessed their fellow travellers in First Class as one of them transpired to be the judge due to hear the very case they were discussing. The trial never took place, and the loud-mouthed businessmen were lucky not to have spent time in prison. Hennessey was released but found the city too hot to return to for a long time.

Most of the businessmen involved remain established figures of the local community. They live in big houses, enjoy expensive holidays and drive much desired cars. For me though they are just the mirror image of low life criminals. Emaciated drug addicts entering peoples' homes at night in order to steal are just the downside of opportunity and the upside is the business world. There are good and bad in all walks of life with the majority of people falling between the two and that applies to the Police just like the whole of society.

During the first part of my police career, I had viewed the World in a very different way. I believed I was on the side of good trying to hold back the forces of the bad. As I rose through the ranks experience made things seem greyer and greyer. Hopefully telling the tale of my years as a senior police officer will not cause too much anguish, but I do believe I have a story to tell.

CHAPTER TWO

RESEARCH SERVICES

Apart from a year spent at the Police Staff College, Bramshill, the first eight years of my career had been of an operational nature. I had found a considerable degree of job satisfaction and happiness when working as a uniform shift inspector, responsible for two sergeants and ten constables on a day-to-day basis. However, for various reasons I decided that the time had come to seek out a post based at Force Headquarters.

The first Headquarters job that became vacant was that of Inspector, Research and Services Branch. I had no real idea what that involved. I knew no one who worked there, nor anyone who ever had. If I mentioned applying for the post to anyone, then the comment would be something like, "Ah! The Ivory Tower" or "Boffins. Not real Coppers!"

I was invited for an interview, and I cannot now remember what I was asked about. I do remember that the whole process felt uncomfortable and I left feeling that I would need to keep looking for the Headquarters Post I was after. Within two days I received a report telling me that I had been successful, and I was to start in my new job within two weeks. The elation at having got what I wanted did not last long. No one else had applied and the interview had been a formality. Further, the more I thought about it, I was not sure if I really wanted it!

There was, however, no way out. I was committed. This was to be a major changing point in my career, and it took me way out of my comfort zone. Maybe everyone should be made to do that once in their lives. I am not certain I enjoyed the experience, but it opened up lots of doors which came later.

The Research and Services Branch was based in a rented building; built in the 1960's of glass and concrete, it was very hot in summer and very cold in winter. I shared an office with another inspector, Mick Hewson. He was a short man, almost bald but with a thick and scruffy beard. In his uniform shirt and trousers, you would still struggle to identify him as a police officer.

Mick Hewson was undoubtedly eccentric. His role was to liaise with the Information and Technology Department and, unlike most police officers at that time, he could speak the language that the 'geeks' did. He looked for ways of using new technology in a police setting and then asked the 'geeks' if they could deliver it. Looking back to 1986 it is amazing how few people understood computers, even mobile phones were then on a par with space travel.

On one occasion, when I had been in Research for a while, I received a phone call to say that our Chief Superintendent was to visit. We nicknamed that individual the 'Red Leader' (I do not know why), he had a habit of arriving for a chat and managed to leave lots of work when he went. By the time you had finished the work he had forgotten what he had asked you to do and had moved onto his next idea.

I informed Mick that he was coming and that triggered a rush of activity that indicated he was going out in order to avoid the proposed meeting. He opened the wardrobe to get his coat and as he did, so we heard Red Leader coming down the corridor. It was too late for Mick to get out of the office so, to my amazement, he got into the wardrobe just as the office door opened.

Red Leader was a tall slim man with thinning, fair hair. He wore tired looking suits that had once been expensive, and he always looked as exhausted as the suits did! I made him a cup of coffee and he opened a window before getting his cigarettes out. He then stood next to the window and smoked one cigarette after another which he lit from the previous one. The stub of each cigarette was flicked out of the window into the street below.

Red Leader had the habit of beginning every conversation by criticizing a long list of fellow officers. He then informed his current audience that he held them in high esteem. They would be described as his elite team who he would look after. Initially this approach worked well with me but, over time, continued exposure to his strategy revealed the flaw. Those whom I had heard condemned suddenly became part of his elite inner sanctum while the former elite would be described as 'rubbish'. Clearly, he used the same technique on everyone and in the end, I just switched off and let it flow over me.

I am sure that beneath the veneer there lurked a decent man, but he was totally self-absorbed. Just before Christmas he asked a female researcher to go and buy a present for his wife. He also asked her to get some 'girlie magazines' for 'the house'. (By that he meant those glossy magazines that feature model homes, expensive clothes etc....not the type most often found in sleezier shops)

"I have no idea what she wants." He declared. "She'll get me some socks or some such rubbish. I've got drawers full. I forgot hers last year. All the bloody relatives will be round as well, so you best get some 'sweeties."

The researcher had no idea what to get or how much to spend and this appeared to amaze Red Leader as the researcher was a female too. In the end it was decided that a "frock or something" should be purchased and a roll of ten-pound notes was handed over. He seemed to have no idea what money was worth or how much he had.

Soon after that Christmas, I had hurt my back in a rugby match and when I informed Red Leader about this, he announced that he thought he had a heat lamp. He drove me to his home address, which was about ten miles from where we worked, and when we arrived, he took me upstairs and let down some steps leading into the loft. As we climbed the steps, I saw that the loft resembled a Father Christmas's Grotto. It was full of boxes, many still in Christmas or birthday wrapping paper.

Red Leader began opening the parcels and revealed among other things an electric drill and a coffee percolator. Finally, he found what he was looking for, wrapped in paper adorned with penguins and bearing a card that said, "With love from Chris." He handed me the box and his only comment was,

"Please do not bring the bloody thing back!"

He had no consideration of the thought that went into the buying of gifts for him and no enthusiasm for personal belongings. Anyway, there will be more of Red Leader later but for now I have left Mick Hewson ensconced in the wardrobe, there he remained, until our top manager left when he set off to another meeting an hour later. Mick emerged from his hiding place, almost bent double but with a smile on his face as he had dodged getting more work.

I was left with the task of investigating "a rubbish American idea called 'Crime Screening'". Red Leader had said that I should look at it and then "bin it." So, once again I envisaged a challenging and worthwhile piece of work!

In the 1980's when a member of the public reported a crime they would be visited by a uniform constable. If the crime was straightforward, then the first officer may deal with it. If the 'job' was a burglary or something else complex, then a detective constable would become involved.

By the late 1980's my Force recorded over one hundred thousand crimes in a year for the first time. That sort of number required a lot of visiting and, as some things first thought to be crimes were subsequently declared not to be so, there were many more unproductive visits.

In America some Forces had decided to focus on those crimes where there was a fair chance of detecting them. So, when a member of the public rang up to report a crime the call handler completed a check list. The questions asked included items such as, "Did a witness see the crime committed?'" "Had there been previous crime of the same type?" "Was the offender known to the complainant?" "Was there likely to be any forensic evidence, such as blood or fingerprints?"

These questions led to a "solvability score" and the higher the score the more likely an officer or a detective officer would be sent. A low score would result in a crime being filed at the outset, unless it could later be linked to another solvable crime of the same type.

At the time the idea appealed to me greatly. A large amount of wasted time could be saved, and the saved time could be spent on 'real' work. The best way to sell the theory was to focus on the thefts of bottles of milk from doorsteps. Nowadays, the service that delivered milk to peoples' houses has almost died out, but in the 1980's nearly every house would have two or three pints delivered to the doorstep every day. Children were not into Red Bull or Pepsi Max and the bottles of milk just standing there in the open provided a source of temptation to some of those passing.

So, if the disappearance of a bottle were reported to the police, then a report of crime would be made. A uniform constable would attend and then try and detect it (that is, find out who took it.). If there had been bottles taken from several steps or on several different days, then the CID may also become involved. Pounds were spent attending "crime scenes" where milk worth only a few pence had been taken. These crimes were seldom detected and if they were, then the young person would be cautioned (warned).

It seemed to me that a report could be taken when the victim rang up about the incident. A questionnaire could be completed and if it was one bottle and absolutely no chance of a detection an officer need not be sent. I designed a form that could be used by the call takers that could be added to the computerized crime report. In addition, I conducted a piece of research that revealed that forty percent of crimes would not be visited by a police officer and sixty percent would not be visited by the CID.

Red Leader had told me to 'bin' the idea. I didn't and explained it to the Chief Constable when he made an ad hoc visit to the Research Branch. He liked it! Further, he wanted a presentation to be made to the Police Authority. What had I done? Why had I opened my big mouth? I hated public speaking, and I was terrified of politicians.

The Police Authority was a strange body. It was there to make sure that the local Police Force ran efficiently, and that Chief Officers were kept in check. The Chief Constable had absolute control over operational matters, but the Police Authority kept a finger on the pulse and exercised some control on expenditure. My Chief Constable was in a state of constant battle with the Chair of the Police Authority, and I was led to believe that making a presentation there would be like being thrown to the lions.

I prepared overhead slides and 'hand outs'; further, I carefully drafted exactly what I wanted to say. Eventually the dreaded day came. I drove to the large Council Offices where the Police Authority had its' base. I arrived on time and was asked to sit in a gloomy waiting room until I was called.

An hour later it was my turn. The Meeting Room was large, and wood panelled, with a huge highly polished table standing in the middle. I am not certain what I expected, but this was not it. It resembled a large dinner party with everyone facing inwards.

The Chief Constable was standing at one end of the table. Those round the table were all male, middle aged to elderly and none of them looked particularly pleased to be there. I was beckoned to join the Chief who had told me that he would introduce me. He noticed that I had overhead slides, and he had a quick look at them then asked for the shutters to be closed. As the room was plunged into a gloomy darkness the Chief commenced to display my slides, commenting on each of them. After some time, he sat down telling me he had 'done' the slides so I could just talk and answer questions.

I laid my speech out on the table and then realized, to my shock, that I could not read them in the dim light. I should have asked for the shutters to have been opened but nerves kicked in and I struggled on from memory. I was lost, just like a rabbit caught in a car's headlamps. After less than five minutes the Chief began gesticulating, moving his right index finger round and round, then tapping his watch with the finger. Eventually his arm was flailing round as if he were trying to take off and I gradually realized he meant that I was to wind the presentation up. I stopped almost immediately, feeling as if the whole thing had been a total failure. No one asked any questions, those at the meeting, the ones who were still awake, sat glowering at me. It was over.

If I felt a sense of relief when I escaped from the meeting it did not last long. The following day the local newspaper had an interesting headline. "Police abandon Crime Victims." It related to my presentation and the three or four paragraphs included several critical comments from the Labour councillor who had Chaired the meeting. I felt that the idea would be abandoned immediately and consigned to the bin where Red Leader had first suggested I should send it.

To my amazement an upbeat Red Leader arrived the following day with a smile on his face and two packets of cigarettes. The Chair of the Police Authority did not like the proposal. Therefore, the Chief was determined to go ahead and introduce the system exactly as I had suggested. Red Leader stood there flicking his cigarette stubs onto passing pedestrians while we worked out how to go ahead.

Very soon after the furore caused by the proposal of Crime Screening, the Research Branch became involved in costing and monitoring the service it provided to the rest of the Force. From that relatively small piece of work came the task of providing a costing of all policing services. That was truly mind boggling in those days but is done as a matter of course now.

All the information did exist within the Force but it was in a host of different places. Much of it was recorded manually and kept in filing cabinets, some of it was retained on computers but that was seldom easy to extract in a form that was useful to our purposes. The plan was to get all the information onto one piece of paper where is could be assessed, and accurate comparisons made.

The document which was produced was named the Audit Guide and, yes, it was on one piece of paper though it was a massive piece, about a meter long and the same wide. All the Divisional Commanders and Department Heads were sent copies and a few weeks later we went round to get their views on the document. Most had not looked at it, some gave it to a junior office to comment on, but one or two did at least admit that it could have value.

I attended the Forces' top meeting, which was then called the Policy Group, and it was hysterical to see twenty-five people trying to spread the sheets out on the limited table space. I am certain that a couple of them were looking at the document upside down. The frustration was evident, and it was obvious that another format had to be considered.

A small group of us got together to decide how we could make the Audit Guide more 'user friendly'. We decided that it should be smaller, perhaps it ought to be printed on more sheets and issued in a booklet form; it was also thought that charts, diagrams, graphs and explanations should also be used. Some of us thought that the Force Audit Guide should be a summary of findings while separate Guides should be issued for each area of command.

All the things that we came up with could nowadays be done on a laptop computer but then the task looked monumental. However, there did seem a belief among the team that we could achieve it and we were excited that this was very much new ground in the Police Service.

It was decided by Red Leader that we should apply to the Home Office for a Police Research Grant and a proposal was sent off while we continued to work on the project ourselves. I had drafted an idea of what the finished product would look like. It was done by hand and based on imagined figures, but it looked reasonable, and we were making progress.

Some weeks later we received a letter from the Home Office informing us that we had been awarded a grant of ten thousand pounds. Once again it is necessary to point out that ten thousand pounds may not seem a lot for 'white hot' research but in those days that amount was more than many people worked a full year for. It is also worth commenting on the fact that Chief Officers clearly did not trust the quality of staff they had within the Force; it was decided that the grant would be used on bringing in a consultancy firm.

We asked several firms to tender for the piece of work and eventually a well-known, prestigious company was selected. To those of us working on the Audit Guide we felt like the Seventh Cavalry were about to come riding to our rescue. However, the feeling of elation did not last long. I, for one, was surprised at what we were to get for our ten thousand pounds. In broad terms it was four days research, four days consultancy and two days report writing. A thousand pounds a day! Well, all I could think was they must be good to get away with charging that; the Chief Constable earned three thousand pounds a month for managing almost three thousand people and a budget running into millions.

Anyway, we were assured that we were buying into a cutting-edge piece of work which would be conducted by one of the foremost experts in the field of performance management. We soon received a shopping list from the consultants asking for examples of all the data we held and a technical breakdown of the capabilities of our computers. That piece of work kept us going for nearly a month and then we waited with a sense of nervous excitement.

I had never met a consultant before, and I admit to expecting a smart, well-groomed fairly young person. The man who arrived did not meet my expectation. He was fortyish and to say he was pleasantly plump would have been grossly complimentary. The man before us had greasy, black, curly hair and a dark shadow of stubble covering his chin. The main item of his clothing that I remembered was a crimson waistcoat that stretched almost to bursting point across his large gut. The suit jacket was too small for him, and the trousers were too short.

The consultant, who we will call Larry, was a lively, boisterous type who would probably have been the life and soul of a party. He demanded coffee, lots and lots of coffee. He grumbled that he had underestimated how far we were from London. He grumbled about how the local people spoke, how bad the trains were and how bad he expected the northern beer to be.

When he finished grumbling, he asked for some wastepaper, some cello tape, a cardboard box and a hard back A4 folder. He announced that we were going to bond, and he had us move all the desks, in the open plan office, to the sides of the room. While we moved the furniture Larry rolled up the wastepaper into a ball and used the full roll of cello tape by wrapping it round and round the ball of paper. The box was placed on the floor near to the door and we were then divided into two teams. We were about to play 'office cricket'.

The binder was the bat, the box was the wicket, the cello tape had completed a perfectly usable ball. To complete preparations a typist was called in to keep the score and act as an umpire. Play began at mid-morning and went on until shortly after two o' clock when Larry said he needed feeding. So we took him out for lunch during which he sampled the local beer and found it quite acceptable.

On returning to the office, we thought that work would now commence. However, Larry did not think that we had fully mastered office cricket, so we played it again, and did so till we all went home.

I had assumed that Larry would commence the consultancy in earnest the following morning. However, while we were ready to start, our consultant was late. His arrival, nearly two hours late, was accompanied by another tirade of grumbling. The northern bed was too hard, the northern traffic was too noisy, the northern bacon was too crispy.... on and on. He wanted coffee, lots and lots of it, as before. While he drank his coffee, he told us to roll the cricket pitch while he came around.!

We never really did any work while he was there, nor did we see him do anything particularly onerous. While we played office cricket, he asked the odd question or two. He left at lunchtime on the fourth day, and I reckon he had been there a total of fifteen hours.

I never saw Larry again though he did return to the Force to present his findings to the Chief Officers. The report was a reiteration of what we had prepared for him. To me we had been the victims of 'daylight robbery'. We had paid ten thousand pounds of the taxpayers' money to play cricket and find out exactly what we knew in the first place. My superintendent sought to explain the situation to me; we were minions who were not trusted to produce anything meaningful, but the consultants had given our work the stamp of approval and we could get on and do what we wanted.

The only lasting value of the consultancy to us in the office was that when we got fed up, we played cricket—the consultant said we should.

I have never been comfortable with the idea of paying vast amounts of money to consultants. More recently the consultancies that have been commissioned into the National Health Service must have cost millions of pounds and I would love to know where the value was added. You can buy a lot of aspirins for fifty pence, but the NHS pay pounds for every prescription.... perhaps I should start a consultancy.

However, the biggest waste of money I have ever been involved in was a team bonding session for the Force Senior Management Team. There were thirty people in the dining room of a large hotel. We were given a list of characteristics and we had to pick three that we thought we possessed. Around the room were Chief Officers who had lists of their characteristics on boards in front of them. You had to go and join the Chief Officer with the characteristics nearest to your own.

The Chief Officers had to engage with you so that you remained, rather than leaving and moving somewhere else if you wanted to. One Chief Officer lay under a large duvet where it was warm, and he invited those who joined him to get under it with him; another fed his team chocolates to keep them; another handed out pens and pencils.

I am not certain what the Chief Officers were trying to achieve. Perhaps they were trying to be nice for once or to show that they could be charismatic. However, every senior police officer knows that you cannot polish a turd and I would not have joined the Deputy Chief Constable (at that time) if he had been giving away ten-pound notes….at that time I had reasons for believing him to be the most odious individual you could hope to meet, chocolates or not.

The Audit Guide did develop over the years and in its' early days it threw up some interesting anomalies in resourcing and performance. The Chief Officers who had commissioned the Audit Guide did not really believe in it and they paid lip service at best, but we were about to get a new Deputy Chief Constable who would change all that.

CHAPTER 3

MORE 'RED LEADER' AND ERROL FLYNN

I had never given much thought to Chief Constables and their other Chief Officers. As a constable I could barely recognize one of the Assistant Chief Constables; they were extremely remote figures and I seldom saw one.

Not long after I joined the Force I was sent on a short attachment to the Warrants and Summons Office. I became friendly with one of the officers working there and I accompanied him on duty a number of times. Weeks later, as I approached the east side entrance of the Force Headquarters building, I saw someone struggling to unlock the door. When I arrived at the door, I thought the man there was the officer from my time in Warrants and Summons. I got my box key out (a key which opened Yale locks on all police buildings) and said,

"You'd think that lot upstairs could afford to get better locks!"

"Yes. You would, wouldn't you." Replied the man.

As we entered the building another officer on his way out said.

"Good morning. Sir."

The man replied with his own greetings and dashed off up the stairs. I suspected I had mistaken the man's identity and later discovered he was the Assistant Chief Constable (Operations).

I was, therefore, not that interested when we were told that we were getting a new Deputy Chief Constable. The old one had been in post for years and I had only spoken to him twice. However, this new one was to make a bigger impact on me.

His arrival was quite dramatic. I wish I could have witnessed the event in person. I heard two different versions and I suppose the truth will be somewhere between them.

Early one morning a tall, solidly built constable was walking along in the yard at the back of the Force Headquarters. That yard had an open gate at each end and a one-way system was operated through it. The constable was approaching the east gate which was the exit from the yard. Suddenly, a sleek black Porsche swept into the yard through the exit. It surprised the wandering constable who had to jump out of the way.

Recovering his composure, the constable followed the car to where it was being parked. As the driver emerged from the vehicle the officer said,

"Who the fuck do you think you are? Fucking 'Night Rider."* (*a character from a TV series.)

The driver was familiar with the programme and seemed amused by the analogy.

"No." He replied. "I'm your new Deputy Chief Constable."

That is the version of the event as it was recounted by the Deputy at a management meeting, and it fitted closely with that told by a civilian member of staff who was present at the time. However, the constable, who was also quite high in the Mormon Church, denied having used bad language.

Our new Deputy was a distinguished looking man. He was about six feet two inches tall and greatly resembled the actor Errol Flynn with his thin moustache and well-groomed appearance. There are going to be several Deputy Chiefs and Chief Constables in these pages, so we will call this one Ronald.

Research Services and Development was under his command, and he quickly decided that he would use the Audit Guide as the basis for his inspections of the Force. He asked me to draw up packages in a clear and usable form. The consultancy paper had not been with the Force for long and little progress had been made with computerizing the new format. So, I produced the documents by hand. There were all sorts of graphics, comparators, performance indicators and a whole section on the demographics of the area being inspected (population, economy, industry etc.)

The Deputy seemed to like what I produced, though he insisted that the documents were kept to ourselves before the inspections. I suppose that this enabled the questions and format to come as a surprise to those being inspected. I was regularly phoned or visited by senior officers from Divisions and Departments that were about to have an inspection. All sorts of promises and threats were made in order to have a glimpse at the reports, but I knew that any favouritism would have been the end of my time with the Deputy. Indeed, one of the first inspections I did with my new boss could well have been the last and the events on that day went something like this.

I had driven Ronald to two previous inspections in his staff car, however, on the third occasion he had another appointment first and he told me he would make his own way there. I could travel direct without first visiting Headquarters and it seemed like it would be a leisurely start to the day.

At the time I was living in a small cottage in a village near the coast. It had become a routine that once or twice a week I took my dog to the beach for a run before I went to work. I then collected driftwood to take home for my wood burner.

The later start for my day meant a perfect chance for a beach visit. My car was an old Austin Maxi which had a zero score on the 'street cred' ratings, but it was very reliable and extremely functional. I could put the back seats down and use it as an estate car which held lots of firewood.

The dog, a black and white cocker spaniel called 'Mugsy', liked to sit on the front passenger seat and would eat an apple on the way home from the beach.

On this particular day the sun was shining, and I enjoyed the run on the soft compacted sand. I then made a pile of wood for loading before driving my car onto the beach and it was only then that I realized Mugsy was not to be seen. I called and called but there was no sign of the dog running up with his tail wagging as usual. I began to get pangs of guilt as I had run and done the wood collecting without taking much notice of him. Then as I began to search, I saw a large, dark, long object lying on the sand near the incoming sea. As I approached the object, I realized it was the carcass of a large basking shark and to my amazement the shark seemed to be moving.

As I arrived next to this long dead and very smelly shark my dog suddenly burst out from inside it. Mugsy was covered in entrails and putrescence having burrowed into the decaying creature. My dog trotted up to me appearing very proud of himself, but the smell was repulsive. I picked him up and took him to the edge of the sea and threw him in; when he emerged and finished shaking, I wiped the remnants of shark off him. There was no time to do more, I had to get home, shower and set off to work. Leisure was now out of the window; it would be a rush just to get everything done and to the inspection on time.

The car steamed up and I had to put the heater on to clear the windscreen. The stench was unbearable, but the dog just lay there on the passenger seat munching his apple and with an appearance of total contentment radiating from him.

As I was now running late there was no time to unload the wood and no time to fill up with fuel at the Petrol Station. I could clean the car and get fuel when the days' work was over. The frantic journey to meet the Deputy got me there just in time and after briefing him the inspection went well to begin with.

The Deputy was due to meet two sergeants and it was then that things started to go off track.

"Weren't you in my earlier Force?" My boss asked a dark-haired, middle-aged sergeant.

"Yes, Sir. You were in charge of Training when I was working there." Came the reply.

"I remember you. They were good days, weren't they? Whatever happened to that attractive blond with the massive tits?"

The sergeant seemed unperturbed and replied, "I married her, Sir."

For the only time during the whole period, I worked for him, Ronald was thrown off his stride. I was about to be thrown out of mine!

"Ah! Yes. Right. Thank you, gentlemen. Very good. James, will you take me back to Headquarters?"

I was as ruffled as he was. Perhaps I should have explained but you didn't normally say "No" to Deputy Chief Constables. I had a car full of drift wood, I was down to fumes in the petrol tank and the car stunk of decaying fish. This was about to be very different than being driven in a Staff Car.

The Deputy Chief Constable was in full uniform and I have to say he cut an impressive figure. You could see yourself in his highly polished shoes, he was immaculate. I expected him to turn his nose up at the Maxi. I certainly expected him to comment on the smell and the wood but he gave no sign of noticing. When I braked hard at some traffic lights a piece of wood shot from the back of the car and landed in the Deputy's lap, he calmly picked it up and put it back over his shoulder.

To my utter relief I got back to Headquarters without running out of petrol. I pulled up near the rear entrance and the Deputy got out.

"I'll see you later." He said and smiled at me. As he turned and walked away from me, I was shocked by what I saw. The back of the Deputys' jacket was a real mess. It was covered with dog hairs and strange strips of decayed shark flesh. His uniform must have stunk when he entered the heat of his enclosed office, but my lasting impression of this episode was the apple core dropping from the back of his trousers as he entered the building.

With a lesser man that could have been the end of my career and a return to operational duties. To his great credit the event was never mentioned and did not appear to impact on our working relationship.

In the early days of my working with the Deputy I thought I had finally found a new role model. He was imaginative, knew what he wanted and would spend time talking to you and sharing confidences as if you were an old friend. I would have worked round the clock for him.

Others did not seem too enthusiastic about him. The Chief Constable certainly did not seem keen to have this dynamic, reforming force undermining his established order. To begin with there was an altercation between the two Chief Officers about where the Deputy would live. Ronald had an old, restored farmhouse in the Pennines and he had no desire to give up living there, his wife also ran a business not far from their family home. The Chief wanted his Chief Officers to show their commitment by moving into the Force area.

There were numerous, often heated, discussions between the two about the issue. In the end a compromise was reached. The Deputy was to give up his Rent Allowance (paid to police officers to help with their rent or mortgages if they did not reside in a police house) and take up residence in a police house in the Force area. The question would be whether or not the Force had a house suitable for the Deputy Chief Constable.

After a protracted search the Deputy identified a house near the border of our Force and very near to the motorway that led to his farmhouse. The house was a pleasant three-bedroom detached property, though unfortunately it was then occupied by a constable and his family.

I am not sure whether the constable moved out voluntarily or was pressurized into doing so. In any event the house was vacated. The Force agreed to fund an extensive redecoration programme and eventually the Deputy had the keys.

Now what happened next is shrouded in the mists of time. It is unclear whether the Deputy actually moved into this newly decorated house. What is certain is that he had not been resident in the house for some time when an old lady rang to express concern about the property, there was water coming under the front door.

The house was soaked and could not be lived in following a pipe burst. What was said between the Chief and his Deputy will no doubt remain a secret. I do know that the Deputy continued to commute on a daily basis. He often found a reason to visit his old Force or somewhere nearby. So, if he was travelling for business purposes, he could claim first class rail return even if he travelled by his car. The nearest town to his house could not be reached in a first-class carriage, so he approached the Police Authority and got permission to claim three second class singles. Many Chief Officers became imaginative when claiming expenses.... though my first Chief Constable certainly did not.

My view of the Deputy was a little tarnished by two incidents that took place in close proximity to each other. In the first case I was personally involved. It had been decided that the new Policy Monitoring and Inspection Branch, which had grown from the old Research Services Department, would go to the Police Staff College for a team building exercise.

Those attending included Red Leader, who was still my direct line boss, three other police officers and three civilian members of staff. This was to be an expensive and hopefully worthwhile venture. We were due to depart from Force Headquarters at 10am as the journey to the College would take at least four hours. The plan was to have a meeting at the College before going out for dinner.

Everyone assembled on time, and we waited and waited and waited. We were all used to waiting for Chief Officers but by noon it looked unlikely that we could get to the College in time for the proposed meeting. An hour later the Deputy emerged from his office and announced that he would travel in his own car and take Jane with him. Jane was an attractive, twenty-one-year-old graduate who had just joined the Branch as a research assistant. She was a little apprehensive at being picked out for this special travel arrangement.

The rest of us set off and had a steady journey to Hampshire. There we unpacked the cars and waited again. By six o' clock in the evening it was obvious that there would be no meeting that day. An hour later we set off to the restaurant where we had booked the evening meal.

The Deputy and Jane arrived at nine o' clock. For some reason I remember that he had mussels for his main course, but I cannot remember what we talked about, it certainly was not work. The following morning Ronald announced that he had to return to the Force and he left immediately after breakfast. He left Jane to travel back with us and she gave us an account of the journey she had the previous day. They had meandered through central England, largely on minor roads and had stopped at two or three country pubs. The Deputy had behaved in a totally proper manner but seemed unwilling to talk about work.

As we had now lost the person who had called the meeting and intended to lead the discussion we also returned to the Force. The meeting never took place and I just got on with my job. Two days were totally written off for a round journey of over five hundred miles, it just seemed really strange, even inexplicable.

The next story did not involve me directly---thank goodness!

The Force had a computerized Crime Information System that had been state of art a couple of years previously but was now creaking at the seams under the volume of crime and the tasks the system was being asked to perform. We were tied to one company, and they were keen that they kept our business which had already run into millions of pounds.

The computer company had a large complex in the south of France where they held courses and hosted hospitality sessions for customers and potential customers. Inevitably an invitation made its way to our Force, and it was decided that the Chair of the Police Authority, the Deputy and Red Leader would attend.

It was a three-day trip involving flights, accommodation, food and generous leisure time. The flight was from a London airport and the journey from Headquarters to the point of departure went without hitch. On arrival, the travelling threesome had some time to kill before their flight and decided to entertain themselves in the First-Class Lounge. Unfortunately, the flight was a charter and not First Class, therefore, staff were reluctant to admit the party. The Deputy explained who he was, stressed the importance of the Chair of the Police Authority and seemed to suggest that Red Leader was some sort of bodyguard. Reluctantly they were admitted to the First-Class Lounge where they enjoyed the free coffee, newspapers and cakes. Red Leader had been asked to listen out for calls announcing their flight and the minutes ticked away comfortably.

Having heard very few flights called, Red Leader went to check their departure time and was shocked to find that their flight had in fact departed on time. I can imagine the horror and panic that my boss must have felt. He had listened carefully but never heard any information about their flight. The Deputy was apoplectic and after venting his wrath on Red Leader he launched a vitriolic attack on the nearest airport staff.

Almost sarcastically the staff were able to inform the Force party that charter flights were not announced in the First-Class lounge. I assume that there would have been a fair degree of embarrassment floating around in the vicinity of the Deputy. Red Leader was immediately dispatched to secure three tickets on the next flight to the South of France.

Four hours later they took off and arrived very late in the day. The computer company agreed to pick them up, but it would be some time. Red Leader told me that they decamped to an expensive restaurant where the Deputy ordered a meal in French. Let us say that two of them did not want the meal that consisted mainly of mussels!

I later saw pictures of the centre that our intrepid flyers eventually arrived at. I would have happily walked to the South of France to have the chance of stopping somewhere like that. The company kept our business.

If the Deputy felt a little lonely in the Chief Constables' team, he was soon to be joined by a colleague from his former Force. The new arrival had little to endear him to anyone. He joined as an Assistant Chief Constable and in time became Deputy when his 'chum' moved on to greater things.

As newcomers the Deputy and Assistant seemed quite close. They jogged together on a lunchtime and usually supported the same motions at meetings. One person who openly despised both of them was the Chief Constables' secretary and she did everything she could to embarrass the Deputy. One particular trick required an incoming phone call, and it followed the same pattern.

The Deputy was, as I have already indicated, very much concerned about his appearance and grooming. His office was also immaculate, and one wall was largely covered by an expensive oil painting borrowed from the City Art Gallery. It was all part of his flamboyant, show man style of management.

The Deputy tended to keep the door to his office open and in consequence the Chiefs' secretary often called across the corridor to him rather than phoning. The office also had its own toilet, wash basin and mirror so he seldom needed to emerge. If there was a phone call for him the secretary would call and if he did not reply then the secretary would say to the caller,

"He's on the toilet. It could be some time."

This picture of a six-foot two man sat on a toilet with his trousers round his ankles and obviously with some sort of problem did not fit with the image which the Deputy carefully cultivated. Sometimes the secretary would use a different approach, she would simply say, "he's preening himself." I am not certain that that was any more positive!

In spite of revealing the downside of the Deputy I must say that he never did me any harm. In many ways he was a breath of fresh air, and he went on to become a good Chief Constable in another two Forces. For me the image became a little tarnished when you were exposed to him for too much time.

He would share his inner most thoughts and secrets with you and divulge details of his early life and career. To believe that such a person would share that with you made you want to achieve miracles for him. Then when you heard that he had shared the same information with umpteen others, you were left with the feeling that your relationship with him was just based on froth.

However, I was spending more and more time with Red Leader and his man management style was even worse. He also liked to engage you in intimate and secretive discussions and as I have said he would then criticize other work colleagues. The next step was to tell you how lowly he regarded them and how highly he thought of you. Only when the colleagues discussed with you that he had said about you it become obvious that he had the same tactic with everyone.

Red Leader was obsessed with work and had little life away from the Police. For years he never took a day off for a holiday or because of illness, until at last his wife put her foot down. They were to go to Tuscany and several hotels in romantic locations were booked. No one believed that he would actually go, but in the end, he surprised us all.

I had been to Tuscany and loved the place so when he arrived back at work, I asked him if he had enjoyed himself. His response was something like this.

"What a smelly place. Anyway, I met a chap who was high up in the management of Boots and we got talking about management by objectives. We sat by the Arno and worked it all out with a stick in the mud. I've got it all on a fag packet.

Anyway, I was thinking about your career, you're too bright to be stuck here. One day I said to Brenda, 'look, I have to go and think about James' career.' So, she got out of the car in Florence, and I drove off. It was only when I got back to the Hotel that I realized I had left her miles from there. I had to buy her a frock to make it up with her. I was glad to get back home. I didn't take to Italians; I couldn't understand them. She won't get me on holiday again."

Even if there was only an atom of truth in Red Leaders monologue, I could sympathise with his long-suffering wife. I do not know if Red Leader ever anything did to help my career, but I was soon to move on. I became Staff Officer to the Chief Constable; I really was entering the inner sanctum.

CHAPTER FOUR

STAFF OFFICER

When I became his Staff Officer the Chief Constable had held that rank and post for twelve years. He must have been one of the most experienced Chief Constables in the country and had been responsible for coordinating the police response during the Miners' Strike. There was undoubtedly a lot of envy and jealousy between Chief Constables. The size of a Force, the buildings and equipment it possessed all led to a sense of rivalry.

At a meeting of the Association of Chief Police Officers (ACPO) one of the senior Chiefs arrived in a brand-new Jaguar staff car. At lunch time he was showing his colleagues around the car, and he pointed out that the vehicle was fitted with a car phone. This was in the days long before mobile phones and the ability to talk from a car to a land line or similarly equipped vehicle was state of the art.

Envy must have been rife among those given the guided tour. Within four months my Chief had a Jaguar and had had it fitted with a car phone. As he drove to another meeting, he could not resist calling the colleague who had introduced him to the technology. For a few moments the two men chatted away amicably enough, then my Chief became the victim of a finely honed put down.

"Bob, I 've got to go. I've got a call coming in on the other line."

At that time our car had only one line, clearly someone was going to suffer for that oversight.

If my Chief was not as well equipped as some of his colleagues, he certainly made up for it with the extra curricula jobs he had acquired. He was an adviser to a multitude of bodies, such as the Association of County Councils and the Association of the Metropolitan Councils. He attended a great many meetings in this advisory role, and this involved a considerable amount of time out of the Force area.

Part of my job was to provide the advice that he passed on to the meetings he attended. I to arrange his overnight accommodation for him and his driver. I also had to complete the expenses claim forms for costs he had accrued when away from home. I wrote speeches that he gave at social functions and public addresses. I also operated as a sort of 'spy in the cab'. When the Chief was away from the Force, I had to keep an eye on what the other Chief Officers were doing and report anything that seemed unusual to my boss.

I also had lots of strange extra jobs which no one had told me about when I took the post. One of those jobs involved me inheriting a pin and a bottle of vinegar to operate on a key piece of machinery. The Chief had a shower and bathroom attached to his office and the water in our Force area was extremely hard and chalky. I had to use the vinegar to break up the chalk in the shower head and the pin was to poke deposits out of the holes.

One of those extra jobs 'bit' me quite early when learning the ropes. On one occasion the Chief had thanked me for two papers I had written for him. He went home in a good mood, and I felt we were developing a good working relationship. The following morning the Chief was late. He hated being late and was difficult to be with when he had arrived late.

The driver had arrived at the Chiefs' address on time, and they had chatted in a relaxed manner as they neared Headquarters. Then they hit road works on a flyover into the city centre. By the time traffic started to move more freely the Chief was almost homicidal, he stormed into the Headquarters building and started shouting my name as he came up the stairs.

"Marchbank, you are a bloody idiot."

"Sir?"

"The bloody road works. You should have told me. That is your job!"

I wanted to speak. I wanted to say something like,

"Yes. It must be my job along with washing your socks and scrubbing your back."

But I didn't say that I just let him rant and rave until, like a storm, the tantrum just died out. It was one of those things that I worked with and through. I hit on the ideal management solution for checking roadworks in future, I delegated the job to the driver who in turn requested a daily report from the Force Control Room....out of such panics are systems born.

The Chiefs' secretary was devoted to him. I never once heard him raise his voice with her and in most ways, she ran his office. She even instructed fairly senior officers as to what they should say when they had meetings with the Chief. In this way things proceeded smoothly from one day to another and she even bullied the secretaries of other important figures who the Chief wanted to meet. The secretary made sure they almost always came to him rather than the other way round.

She certainly helped me because she 'told tales' to the Chief about his other Chief Officers. That was really my job, but she usually got to him first and those exposed knew who the real spy was.

Shortly after I became the Chiefs' Staff Officer, the Deputy I had worked for departed for pastures new. He took up the post of Chief Constable in a neighbouring Force. I would miss him, largely because I enjoyed working with him but also because his successor was a strange man.

I was not supposed to fill in the expenses claim forms for Chief Officers other than the Chief himself. The new Deputy, let's give him a name too and he can be Brian, knew this as well as I did, but he still regularly asked me to do so. The situation was made worse by his trying to claim for things that were not allowable. Alcohol with meals, newspapers and journals, tips and gratuities these and many other items had to be paid personally by the claimant. Again, I knew the Deputy would know this and by asking me to fill the forms in he obviously hoped I did not know or would be intimidated by his rank. If I put the items through and they were paid then he got the money, if they were picked out during an audit it would be my fault as I had submitted the form.

The Chief would sometimes send me to Marks and Spencer's to buy mussels or smoked salmon. These items would always be for dinner parties he held at his home for work acquaintances, and I was more than happy to run those errands. The Deputy felt he could use me in a similar way and once sent me for a second-hand part for his sons' car. I trailed around scrap yards for three hours before finding what was wanted and getting the money from him was like extracting blood from a stone. I was constantly on edge whenever the Deputy called me to his office and there will be more of him soon.

Whenever I wrote a speech for the Chief I tried to put in a joke or lighthearted anecdote. The serious bits of the speeches he left alone but he always changed the joke, and he always used the same one, which went something like this.

"Running my Force must be one of the hardest jobs I have done. I had a dream in which I had died and gone to heaven. There I met St. Peter and he decided there was still work for me on earth, so he sent me to empty Rotsea Bay using a jam jar. After spending several years trying to empty the Bay by removing jam jar full after full jam jar I was called back to the Pearly Gates where St. Peter greeted me again. 'Bob, I want you to go back to your old Force and sort that out.' I thought about it for a few minutes and then I had to say, 'Look Peter, if its' all the same with you, I'll just go back to working with the jam jar. It's a whole lot easier."

Sadly, running our Force was about to blow up in the Chiefs' face and it was to be expenses and not the big issues of running a Force that crept up and bit him. I would say now that my Chief was one of the most honest people I have ever met. He did nothing which in any way could be construed as dishonest and I will return to the events shortly. However, there had been twelve Chief Constables of the City by the time my Chief took up post. Four of those could be categorized as dodgy or even worse.

The first Chief let it be known that he had held a commission in the Forces, though there is no record of his ever having held one. It was alleged that he took advantage of the wife of one of his officers, but the Watch Committee (the then Police Authority) decided that the allegation was unfounded, even though the Chief was never called to give evidence. A second Chief faced allegations of dishonesty by retaining fees and fines which came into his possession and after admitting having appropriated a substantial sum he resigned and asked for a pension. The full town council were not prepared to let the

Chief escape Scot free and ordered the Watch Committee to withdraw their acceptance of his resignation. Clearly the council wanted some sort of disciplinary action. It is unclear from existing documents if the situation was ever properly dealt with. In reality he agreed to pay back an amount of money and he slipped into history and a new Chief was appointed.

The third Chief was a formidable policeman, but he also lapsed. Prostitution was rife at the time and councillors regularly pushed for more action against prostitutes and brothels. The age of consent for sex had recently been raised from thirteen to sixteen. There was a complaint from the mother of a fourteen-year-old girl that the Chief had entered her house when she was away and had kissed her daughter, asked to see the girls' legs and pulled up her dress before putting his tongue in her mouth. He started to unbutton his trousers but apparently changed his mind and gave the girl six pence and told not to tell her mother. The Watch Committee were in a predicament. They were satisfied that a trial would not result in a conviction, as it would be the Chiefs' word against the girl. They did, however, want the Chief to resign but were worried about the ethics of punishing someone who could not be proved guilty. Fortunately for them the Chief agreed to resign if they gave him three months' pay as he was 'without funds'.

A later Chief Constable who had already served in that rank in Chesterfield came to have a reputation which can best be described by a police officer who knew him well, "he was like the church spire of the borough he had come from." He quickly established a circle of friends from the sleazier parts of the city and undoubtedly benefited from that group and all sorts of allegations of graft and corruption were rife.

He liked to drive into neighbouring Force areas to see what he could 'collect'. On one occasion he wanted a Christmas tree but was disappointed when the woods in the nearby Force only had trees that were too large. The story is recounted that a surprised gamekeeper came across the Chief Constable standing on the shoulders of his driver, busily sawing off the top from one of the trees!

Unfortunately for the Chief he made an enemy of a veteran local politician who campaigned for his removal. All sorts of allegations were made based on the misuse of police cars, the theft of petrol and other such offences. On one occasion the chairman of the Watch Committee was going to Blackpool on holiday and missed his coach. The chair rang the Chief who sent him a car which picked him up and chased the coach

The Home Office held an investigation into the Chief Constable and sent its' report to the town council. The report was not published and indeed its publication was banned until 2027, which seems rather strong stuff if the allegations really did only relate to the misuse of police vehicles!

In light of this sort of 'goings on' what had my Chief managed to do. Was he a sinner of the same ilk as his forerunners? My view is that the Chiefs I have mentioned above represent the bad and the dodgy of policing but in my opinion the Chief I worked for was, if anything, too much of a good guy.

If they were honest, most Chief Officers would say that away trips are very much a gravy train. Okay, some of them would suggest they would sooner be at home but if they are away, they are on a first-class junket. The best hotels, the best food, first class train tickets, business class on planes all very nice and all at the public expense. Things may have changed since my day, especially after the cuts of recent years, but I would need some convincing.

The man I worked for did not fit the mould. He spent a lot of time in London in his capacity as an advisor to several organisations and he also attended the Association of Chief Police Officers meetings which were held there. Most weeks he would be in London for at least two days and more importantly two nights. The cost would or could have been phenomenal, but the Chief had his own way of arranging things. He had become a member of a gentleman's club and he paid an annual fee for the use of the clubs' facilities.

The facilities included overnight accommodation. The room rates were lower than London Hotel prices and there were three different types of room. There were singles, small doubles and large doubles. The singles were rarely available though they were about a third of the price of a London Hotel, the small doubles were about half the price of the London rate and the large doubles were about three quarters of the price of a similar room in a hotel. The Chief, or his Staff Officer, would check if a single were available and if not, a small double would be booked. Often when the Chief arrived, he would be upgraded at no extra charge and if his wife accompanied him on official business, he booked a large double.

The Chief did ask if the Police Authority were happy to pay his annual club membership but when they declined, he continued with the same arrangement and the Force saved a small fortune over time. All that information about rooms is by way of background, but a mistake was made in a claim for the Chiefs' expenses. An auditor discovered a discrepancy, fortunately from a time before I became Staff Officer, and the story was something like this.

The discrepancy related to a time when the Chiefs' life was in turmoil. He had attended the annual Conference of International Chief Police Officers in the United States and like all other delegates he was accompanied by his wife. While they were in America the Chiefs' wife nearly died following a heart problem. The couple remained after the conference finished and his credit card paid for medical treatment, accommodation, food, transport and a host of sundries. I am sure that at a time like that most people would not be thinking about what they could claim, but the Chief did keep receipts and submitted his credit card statements and, on his return, handed the lot to his then Staff Officer.

Completing that expenses claim would probably have needed an accountant to work out what could and could not be claimed at different times and in different places. For example, all food for both of them would be claimable until the conference finished but once the wife was ill and not at the conference could food still be claimed for her? It was a nightmare, both emotionally for the Chief and for the Staff Officer who had to wade through the details of the claim.

I am not certain what was claimed that should not have been, but the mistake had been the Staff Officers, however, the form was signed by the Chief, and it was his claim.

Now, I have already said that the Chief was if anything 'too good'. He was very concerned about being seen to be whiter than white. He was told that there would be an inquiry and his world seemed to fall apart. This was a man who seemed to be heading for a knighthood and now suddenly seemed to have his private life examined in the media.

The whole business of the London claims and which room was used or claimed for reared its' head and investigators were sent to the club. His reputation was being smeared by implication. The Chief considered resigning, but the Force Solicitor said he should let the inquiry take its' course and clearly state that an honest mistake had been made.

The Chief was clearly ruffled by what was going on and he decided to take a period of leave while he made his mind up what to do next. In the Chiefs absence his Deputy moved into the Chiefs' office. This was followed by an outward change in his interpersonal behaviour. I do not know if what followed was a charm offensive or there was a real change by a man who was now contented with his newfound power. Whatever did cause the change in him it had little effect upon the Chiefs' secretary. She did not like the new version any more than the old one. One day she called me into her office which had a door leading into the Chief Constables' suite.

"Look through the keyhole." She said.

I bent and put my eye to the keyhole and had a fairly good view into the Chiefs' office. There at ten o' clock in the morning sat the Deputy with a glass of whisky and a decanter on the desk next to him. I didn't quite know how to react, but the secretary seemed elated that she had caught him in the act.

Later the same day the secretary came to tell me that she had just seen the Deputy topping up the whisky level in the decanter with water. She literally dragged me back to the keyhole so that I could see him doing it. As I bent to look through the hole the door opened. A split second later and I would have been caught peering into the room.

"Have you got plenty to do?" He asked and I retreated to my own office.

In retrospect he would probably have been as worried that he might have been caught as I almost had. He seemed to be watching me all the time from that point as if waiting for a reason to get rid of an ally of the Chief. Fortunately, he never got the chance.

While the Chief was away the Deputy met with the Chair of the Police Authority. The two of them must have discussed the Chiefs' position. But for the expenses crisis the Chief could have remained in post for another four or five years. The Deputy was a man in a hurry, and he had clearly taken a liking to the Chiefs' office. The two of them brokered a deal. There would be no inquiry if the Chief were to resign, he would then preserve his pension and be allowed to leave after a period of six months. The Chief would keep face and the Force would not draw the spotlight of criticism onto itself. For the Deputy there would be a vacancy for the Chief post several years sooner than he could have expected.

I wanted to tell the Chief that he was being manoeuvred out and that he should go through the whole investigation process. However, I never got the chance to talk to him before he accepted the deal. The Chief had six months left and, so I supposed, did I. However, the next few months turned out to be quite dramatic.

I cannot remember the exact sequence of events. However, round about the time that the Chief returned, new guidelines came out requiring all ACPO officers to have completed a Strategic Command Course at Bramshill before their next promotion. The Deputy had not attended such a course and clearly would not be in a position to apply for the Chiefs' job on his retirement, another obstacle had been put in his way.

According to the Chiefs' secretary the Deputy had no desire to spend a large chunk of time in Hampshire when so much was happening in our Force. He will have looked at alternatives and he came across a course that was run by the Royal Canadian Mounted Police. The Deputy liked riding, he had taken to attending the Force stables and riding with the Mounted Section.

He asked permission from the Chief and the Police Authority to apply for a place on the course. His report included mention of his having to ride ceremonially if he attended the course and he would need equipping with a riding uniform and helmet. On the basis of what they were told the Police

Authority granted permission with strict conditions on what expenses should be claimed. Flight, course fees and food were to be paid but everything else was to be paid by the attendee.

Attired with his new uniform and riding boots, off the Deputy duly went and peace settled briefly on the Force. The Chiefs' secretary was still on his case. She told me that she had rung the Royal Canadian Police Headquarters, and someone had told her that the Deputy would not be allowed to ride ceremonially or otherwise in public. They were trying to find a slot for him to ride at their riding school but that would be it. Her informant also told her that the course was aimed at middle management rank (around Chief Inspector level) and it was certainly not for the most senior ranks. It seemed to the secretary that the course represented little more than a paid holiday for the Deputy.

I never checked any of this information, the man could be my boss in six months, but I do know what happened next. The Deputy submitted large expenses claim on his return which comprised, in part, of bills for taxis and phone calls. The claim ran into hundreds and the Police Authority had been explicit as to what could be claimed. The Deputy wriggled and jiggled, and no doubt told them he worked for a caring organization which had his family life to the fore of their thoughts. The result was, I guess a draw. Some of the claims were paid and some were written off. I would have been extremely worried if any of his claims had gone through me, and this was the man who had negotiated the settlement of the Chiefs' expenses debacle.

Then one day, completely out of the blue the Chief called me into his office. It was the most personal chat I had ever had with him. He told me that he was promoting me to Chief Inspector, and he wanted me to take up a new post while he was still at the helm of the Force. I did not want to leave my job until his retirement, but he was adamant.

"James, I have no doubt that when I am gone there will be nothing more ex than an ex-Chief Constable. You will be associated with me and will, therefore be viewed with suspicion. You need a clear break from me before the new regime takes over."

The Chief had a clear vision of the future, and I will leap ahead a short time to reveal just how right he was. The Chief left on schedule and his successor arrived the day after the Chiefs' office was vacated. It had been arranged that the ex-Chief and the new one would meet a day later for the former to brief the current post holder. (It should be pointed out that our Brian was unsuccessful in his application for the post. The new Chief was an 'outsider'.)

The secretary told me that my former boss was due to attend Headquarters at ten o' clock on the day in question and I made sure I was there so I could see him again. His words came home to me like a hammer blow. My Chief, and I still call him that, arrived on time. However, he was now a civilian, he no longer had a key to the building, and he had no warrant card. He attended the desk at the front of the Headquarters and waited his turn with those answering their bail, relatives of prisoners and rough sleepers keeping warm.

The officer on the front desk rang the Chiefs' secretary and the latter shouted through to the new Chief that his visitor was here and added that I could go and bring him up. I stepped into a position where I could see through the new Chiefs' open door. He could not see me as he had his feet on his desk and was holding the 'Guardian' newspaper in front of him.

"Let him wait a while and let him know who's in charge now."

My Chief was kept waiting for almost three quarters of an hour. He showed no sign of being treated badly and maybe that meeting had been part of his earlier vision. I never took to the new Chief, as you will see in what is to come, and I certainly missed the old one, a great man and a great loss to the Force.

The Deputy Chief Constable must have resented the fact that he was overlooked for promotion to Chief. He remained Deputy with our Force for some time, and he would clearly have wanted to know why his manoeuvring had not been successful. The secretary told me of the efforts the Deputy had taken to find out what was recorded about him. The outgoing Chief had completed reports on all his senior officers for the new Chief. These assessments were kept in a wooden filing cabinet in the secretary's office. One morning as the Chiefs' secretary came to work early, she heard someone in her office and then what sounded like wood splintering. As she entered the office there was the Deputy with a long flat piece of metal trying to Force the top drawer open. He was caught in the act.

"Have you lost something?" Asked the secretary, as the Deputy scuttled out of the room.

The Deputy was never to be a Chief Constable anywhere. At a later stage he secured another Deputy Chief Constable post in a neighbouring, larger Force. There he became Acting Chief Constable when a vacancy arose and yet again, he was overlooked for promotion. That time he refused to move out of the Chief Constables' office until he was forced to do so and by then his time in the Police was coming to an end.

Just before he left our Force, he attended an "Open Day" at the station to which I had been promoted. The Force Wildlife Officer had a large collection of creatures on display. There were owls, hawks, snakes, mice, rats, ferrets and all sorts of other things. The Deputy made a bee line for the creatures and arrived just as the officer in charge of them was putting away a Boa Constrictor.

The Deputy wanted to be photographed with the large snake but was told that the Boa was a little agitated, another creature was suggested but our Brian insisted. A crowd had gathered round the wildlife display and the outranked officer carefully passed the snake to the Deputy. The Boa looped over the Deputys' shoulder and its' front-end twined round and round his forearm. The rear end of the snake ended up wrapped round the man's left arm and that is where it defecated copiously. A foul stench soon thinned the number of spectators and as the constable took back control of the snake the Deputy left the building.

I was to have five more Deputy Chief Constables and the last one was by far the worst of the lot. His arrival was at least fifteen years in the future, but if I had seen him coming, I would have left before he got there. For now, with a new Chief Constable, I was in a new job, a job I loved.

CHAPTER FIVE

GOING HOME

Moving from operational policing roles to Headquarters is a little like shedding a skin and taking on a new one. It took me several months to adjust to Headquarters. The different pace, the attention to detail and, of course, the differing agendas of the pack of career minded wolves that worked there. I anticipated that there would be a similar transition period going back to an operational sub divisional role, but this proved to be more a fear than reality.

I had worked at the subdivisionto which I was posted by the outgoing Chief Constable. However, that did not give me any sense of comfort. On returning from my Special Course, after a year away from real Policing, I had been pleased to be sent to a subdivision where I had worked. Then the facts that there had been a great change in personnel and a senior officer who made my life a misery had resulted in those days becoming a living hell. This posting was to be an enormous success, in spite of another senior officer, but that is leaping ahead.

The staff at this subdivisionhad hardly changed at all. It had always been a friendly working environment and constables generally wanted to stay when they arrived. To that extent it was like being welcomed back as a prodigal son, but there had been one massive change. The old Victorian station, with its' antiquated cells and facilities, had gone. There was now a brand-new building at a different location and that was shared with the Force Control Room, the Traffic Department, the Accident Investigation Unit, the Operations Planning Unit and an accommodation wing for the Training Department.

Facilities were first class. There was an excellent canteen, a licensed bar and snooker room, meeting rooms, TV lounges, showers; everything seemed to have been catered for. The subdivision had a first-class social club that organized trips and concerts as well as buying DIY equipment that it hired out to members at a minimal cost. There was a real family feeling about the place and the first few days there was like some sort of reunion party.

My boss was an experienced superintendent. He was a stocky, bald-headed Glaswegian with a reddish face and a tendency to perspire. He had a wicked sense of humour and was fascinating to talk to. His easy-going nature shifted to efficient and professional when incidents required that. I remember him telling me that, as a child, he had lived in a tenement in a rough area of Glasgow. One night during the Second World War he was lying in bed when an air raid started. As a little boy it must have been terrifying. Suddenly there was a loud bang and an accompanying flash. He hid under the bed covers but eventually he ventured to look out. One corner of his bedroom was missing, and he had a clear view of a moonlit sky with clouds moving across his field of vision. He was adamant that the damage had been caused by the anti-aircraft guns rather than the enemy.

For several months the superintendent and I were almost inseparable. We opened the mail together, shared the paperwork between us and divided areas of responsibility evenly. Then gradually my boss and mentor started working shorter days and some days he didn't come in at all. He would usually preface his departures with a statement such as. "I've got gardening to do." Or "I've got to give you the chance to fly solo."

I welcomed the chance to look after everything and I really lost track of the number of days that he wasn't there. Then suddenly he was posted to Headquarters and a job that he later told me he hated. To my amazement no one replaced him and there was no indication that I would be taking over officially. Then the new Chief Constable announced that he was going to reorganize the Force. There would be fewer subdivisions and it would be necessary for a large number of our officers to move from their current stations and be transferred to other operating centres. Indeed our sub division was to cease to exist and become a sector commanded by an inspector. I had no idea where I would go, though once this announcement had been made things seemed to go into slow motion. Things went on as they always had, and some started to believe that there would be no reorganization.

The new Chief had not yet found a house for his family, and he was living in the residential block at my station. It was strange having the top man living at your place of work. He sat in the bar on a night and some officers were put off by the Chief Constables' presence when they were drinking and relaxing. However, after a time he became almost invisible, he came into the bar in a shabby cardigan and a pair of slippers and sat there staring into space.

One evening while I was having a drink in the bar, with my girlfriend, the Chief actually joined our group. He mentioned that he would be 'on call' at the weekend (available if an incident occurred requiring a Chief Officer involvement.) and as result would not see his family for twelve days. As a friendly human gesture my partner invited him to join us for Sunday dinner, but he casually rebuffed the offer, and he wandered off to bed.

I was beginning to think that I would not take to the new Chief Constable. My father had an expression that he used to describe people he thought were either untrustworthy, unreliable or generally sleazy. The words he used were, "a dirty underpants man." I knew what he meant by it and I certainly felt similar thoughts about the new Chief, but at this stage I could not quite put a finger on what he did that triggered my feeling. Perhaps he did not take to me; I had been the Staff Officer for his predecessor and had been that officers' last promotion, perhaps there was a trust issue between us.

Then one day, out of the blue, he called me to his office and greeted me like a long lost relative. I just knew he wanted something. At his previous Force he had been given the job of advising a former eastern bloc country in setting up a western style Police Force that could serve a new democratic society. He had pulled a team together prior to his promotion and had made a start on the work but it was a long way off completion when he arrived with us. The team did not travel with him, only one constable was allocated to him, and that officer was for use as an interpreter.

The Chief had been given a lot of questions by the Government of the country in question. The list ranged from how the UK road system was financed to how we ensured vehicles were safe for use. As soon as the questions were mentioned I knew what he had called me for. There was no consideration of the work I had already got, it was simply a matter of, "you've got three days to complete these."

I mentioned the subdivision which I was currently running by myself, and his response was that the subdivision was history and would soon cease to exist. I appreciated what he was saying but the subdivision would still be there in more than three days and there would still be a work force to manage, a workload to be arranged and, most importantly, the local public who needed a service. I tried to make that point to him but instead he offered me a sweetener, when I had completed the questions, I could accompany him to present them in the country he was advising.

I suppose that the bottom line with Chief Constables, when you are of junior rank, is that you do what you are told. I did what I was told. I just about lived at sub divisional Headquarters for three days, did my day job and completed the questions on schedule. The report was over a hundred pages long. I still have a copy, bound and very official looking but it is credited to the Chief Constable. I was not greatly bothered that my name did not appear on the document, I realized I was a bit player in the greater scheme of things. What did bother me was that he never said thank you and I found that he had reneged on his promise for me to accompany him. Those who flew out to present the questions were the Chief, Red Leader and his linguistic constable.

I was left behind with the task of organizing the demise of the subdivisionthat I loved. I had to determine which officers would have to move elsewhere and who would stay. Great joy! At this point I will put that unpleasant piece of work on hold for a moment.

My local pub was run by an eccentric landlord who often drank more than he should. However, his food was excellent,, and his specialities were curry, steaks and lobsters. He often raced the lobsters across the room while taking bets on which one would get to the other side first. The clientele was a little like the landlord. They could be described as 'eccentric Bohemian' or 'Bohemian eccentric'. A large number of the regulars were gay at a time when people were not so open about their sexuality. They were a great bunch of people and brilliant to socialize with.

One of the pubs characters had once been a police constable but had found things a bit too formal, macho and physical for him. When he left the Police, he opened a clothes shop selling designer items to younger, fashion-conscious men. Many of his customers came from the gay community and his shop was something of a social centre. One day he came over to me in the pub eager to pass on a piece of information.

"James, I've met your new Chief. Can you believe it? He's one of us."

"What do you mean 'he's one of us" I asked.

"You know! Bent as a nine-bob note. Just like us."

"He's married with a family". I protested in disbelief.

"You've heard it from the Oracle on this subject. Believe me. I know!"

I asked how he had come up with this revelation.

"Well, he came into the shop and I, you know, sort of greeted him. I said, 'you're new round here' and he told me he was working at the police station."

"Are you sure it was the Chief Constable?" I asked.

"Well, I said to him 'Do you work for James?' and he got on his high horse, and he said, 'He works for me. I'm the Chief Constable.'"

"And how do you know he was gay from that?" I asked.

"I call it Gaydar. You just know if someone is one of us."

Nowadays nobody would blink if a Chief Officer were gay but, in those days, it was a bit of a shock. My Chief had been apoplectic when the then male Chair of the Police Authority walked into a Police Ball hand in hand with his male partner. I was as shocked by this revelation as everyone had been on that night. To the best of my knowledge there is no substantial evidence one way or another. The Red Leader did once start to tell me about strange goings on during the Chiefs trip abroad in his advisory capacity. He said he had been embarrassed by something that the Chief and the constable had got up to and there was a reference to the fact that the constable, six foot two and built like a prop forward, had dyed his hair platinum blond. I remembered how an earlier boss of mine had grilled me about whether or not I was gay. Everything I did at that time triggered another tirade. What did it matter whether anyone was gay or not, the rumour went nowhere. Like him or not I am glad he was spared the persecution of someone homophobic as I had been.

For now, I will go back to the reorganization. I was faced with the horrible task of breaking up a happy contented and professional team. There was no advice from the Personnel Department as to how I should select those officers who would have to move. A Federation (Police Union or staff organisation) representative assured me that whatever I did I would "end up in the shite."

I spent hours with lists of names and personal records. Then I decided that those with the longest service, had families and owned houses locally should all be near the top of the list for staying. By default, I had found the core group for staying and logically those who fitted none of those criteria would be most likely to move on. The problem was that there was still a large chunk of officers in the middle who met some of the criteria but not all.

It was at about this stage in my deliberations that I was visited by a Detective Chief Inspector. He had the names of those detective officers he wanted to remain at the station we were both based at. My response was that they would remain if they met the criteria or 'won the lottery' if they were selected from the middle group.

He flared up, became quite aggressive and very loud,

"You're going to pick names out of a hat."

I assured him that I had not done that, though I did think that that was probably as fair as anything else. He stormed out of my office exuding an air of righteous indignation.

Later the same day I received a phone call from an Assistant Chief Constable.

"Morning James. Please tell me you haven't moved people on the basis of taking names out of a hat?"

I explained that no one had yet been moved. I had a list of criteria, but the process seemed fairest for the middle group if the selection was random. He told me to do nothing yet and he would talk to the Head of Personnel to see if my proposal was a valid technique. So, he was going exactly where my deliberations had started.

Within a day the Assistant came back to me and told me to get on with it. Taking names out of a hat was perfectly acceptable. When I came up with my list for posting I allowed a few days so that people could talk about it amongst themselves. One or two agreed mutual swaps but by and large there was no major grumbling, soon the majority of staff were moving on and still no one had told me what I was going to do.

Around the time that our new Chief arrived the Government commissioned a report on the police rank structure. When the recommendations were published, attached to a paper known as the Sheehy Report, I suffered a severe sense of humour failure. I had slaved away to get promoted to Chief Inspector and now the suggestion was that that rank and the position of Deputy Chief Constable were to be done away with. The author of the report had concluded that deputy posts were not needed, but to me the findings were flawed. For over one hundred and twenty days a year any worker will not be at work and that is without sickness or training courses. For a third of the year important operational decisions had to be made and junior officers looked upwards for advice and guidance. There was also the fantastic experience that deputy posts offered in helping someone learn how to do the substantive job. To me the recommendations were a money saving exercise based on flawed logic.

The Chief Police Officers Staff Association fought tooth and nail against the removal of the Deputy Chief Constable rank, and they quickly won their battle. The Police Federation seemed less committed to fighting for the Chief Inspector role.

The new Chief Constable called me in soon after I had completed my part in the reorganization. He sat there behind his massive desk with a beaming grin on his face. I would be stopping where I was, I would be the new sector commander. That role was, he explained even though I already knew, was an inspector post. My rank, he said, was a fiction and I was just one of his inspectors.

That was the moment when I realized that there was a problem in our relationship. I cannot to this day understand what I did to upset the new Chief. I still feel that if he was not dodgy, he was at best shady and open to a suggestion of unfairness in the way he handled staff. There will be more of him later, but I think it's about time anyone reading this is given the chance of having a smile at some of the characters I worked with.

CHAPTER SIX

CHARACTERS

In some ways the characters who remain the clearest in your memory are those who have played a part in the turning points of your life or have behaved in an eccentric, unusual or amusing way. The Chief Constables, for example, all played a memorable part in my life but those who appear in this chapter fall into the weird and wonderful category.

Paul Hawthorn was a traffic officer. He was part of the fabric of the Traffic Department, and no one seemed to remember when he had not been there. I first met him in strange circumstances which involved my wife to be.

My girlfriend worked as a nanny for an extremely wealthy family who lived in an area that most of us would be frowned at for driving through. The family had six young children, the youngest two of whom attended nursery school.

One morning, driving to the nursery, my wife was stopped for speeding. She remains adamant to this day that she was not exceeding the speed limit with the children in her car. Also in the car was a tray of freshly baked sausage rolls made for an end of term party at the school. Any hard braking would have strewn them across the front seat.

The officer though had the upper hand. He told her she was going at ten miles an hour over the speed limit. Elaborating he told her she would get a large fine and three points. He then inspected the tyres, the lights and the boot before seeing the sausage rolls.

"I'll have some of those." The officer announced.

My wife explained that she had a set number for the school party.

"Well then." The officer said, "If you bring me half a dozen tomorrow, I'll let you off. Is that fair?"

So, my girlfriend agreed, and the officer threatened to find her at her workplace if she did not turn up with 'his' sausage rolls. The following day the sausage rolls were handed over and the officer formally promised that there would be no further action.

About three weeks later I was in the bar at the station with my girlfriend when Paul Hawthorn came in. My girlfriend immediately recognised him. I introduced us to the officer and after an initial period of tension we all had a good laugh about it. I came to like Paul even though he was far from the image of an efficient and impartial police officer.

He had a long-standing animosity towards a local solicitor and whenever the lawyer parked outside the station Paul found a reason to issue him with a ticket. On one occasion the solicitor had parked on double yellow lines, directly outside the station, just as Paul was going off duty. The officer, who had been in civilian clothes, dashed back inside the building put his uniform back on, collected a book of tickets and duly did what he always did to the solicitors' car. Over time Paul issued more than ten tickets to the lawyer and there was a formal complaint, but nothing came of it as no rules or regulations had been broken.

Then one day when Paul was on duty, he saw the solicitor driving on a roundabout whilst eating a chocolate bar. A blue light stop resulted in the lawyer being reported for the offences of failing to exercise proper control over his vehicle and driving carelessly. The incident of the 'Toffee Crisp' became notorious and again resulted in a complaint from the solicitor. On this occasion the powers that be decided that a prosecution was not in the public interest. Paul was furious and vowed to continue his vendetta, but before he had the chance, he indulged in behaviour that nearly ended his career.

Paul was on duty in his traffic car parked near to the police station. He was relaxed and waiting a few minutes before he went in and booked off duty. He was making up his notebook when he saw a black transit van pass his position. A few moments later the van passed him again going in the other direction and then it returned a third time. Paul decided to see what the driver was up to and eventually he stopped the van immediately outside the police station.

The driver and the front seat passenger were of Afro Caribbean origin, and both were heavily dread locked. It quickly transpired that the men were lost, and Paul was about to provide directions when further men in the back of the van became loud and opinionated. Paul says he could not understand a word of what was being said by those in the back of the van and nor could he see them. He later did say that what he heard was something like, "Ra, Ra, Ja, Man Ra."

Unable to quieten the men in the back of the van he went to his car and collected a banana, left over from his lunch, and returned to the van. He went to the back of the vehicle, opened the door, threw the banana in and said, "now then monkeys, behave." Having done this, he set off back to see the driver, but by now all the vehicles' occupants were incensed and getting out of the van. Paul realized what he had done and retreated to the station followed by the six men who collectively formed a Reggae Band.

As you can imagine most people would nowadays condemn Pauls' behaviour as racist. Even in those days Paul realized he had overstepped the mark. I met the men in the foyer of the police station and the men from the back of the van were extremely irate and aggravated. The driver, however, thought the whole episode was hilarious.

Paul was mortified, in large part because he feared he could lose his job. In his defence he said that the men in the back were behaving like naughty monkeys, and he would have thrown the banana in whether they were black or white. I explained what Paul had said about the incident to the band members; they were happy that he had been spoken to and was frightened about the implications of what he had done. However, even though the complainants were happy and regarded the matter as closed, the nature of the event made it unsuitable for it to be resolved informally. The paperwork went to the Discipline and Complaints Department where they decided Paul would be officially reprimanded.

Like a lot of officers Paul sailed close to the wind, he had a wicked sense of humour that either had people in hysterics or shocked disbelief. How some of that group of officers survived amazed me, others came unstuck through no real fault of their own and one of those was 'Lunch Box' Butler.

Lunch Box had joined our Force with previous policing experience gained in Australia. He had emigrated to Australia, but his family did not settle there, and they all returned to the UK after four or five years. During the last week, of his time working as a police officer 'down under,' he had been patrolling in the outback without seeing any vehicles for several hours. Not long before setting off back to his base station he came upon the body of a kangaroo lying in the roadway, so he pulled up and got out to drag the carcass out of the way.

As he got out of his police truck, he saw a sign at the edge of the road. For some reason this sign inspired him to concoct a photograph. He took his leather jacket off and put it on the kangaroo. He then leaned the animal against the sign and put his cap on its' head. Lunch Box went to collect his camera and as he turned round the kangaroo was miraculously hopping off into the scrubland. This was serious because officers had to pay for the expensive leather jackets if they lost them.

Lunch Box had a shotgun in the truck, but the kangaroo was already out of range, so he leaped into the vehicle and set off in pursuit. The truck bounced and lurched its' way over the uneven ground until Lunch Box got near enough to risk a shot. He aimed and pulled the trigger and the kangaroo crashed to the ground. The leather jacket was retrieved from the now definitely dead animal but unfortunately the back of the garment was shredded by the shot and covered in blood.

While aware of the slapstick nature of this incident, Lunch Box was upset at what had happened to the kangaroo. He was, however, extremely lucky to get away with handing in the jacket before leaving Australia for good. He settled into our Force quite quickly, but his luck was due to run out.

When Lunch Box worked a night shift his wife, who was a nurse, invariably worked a day shift. So, when husband came home from a night at work his wife had already left. Lunch Box would make a cup of tea and head for bed, he left the curtains closed knowing that his wife would open them as soon as she returned, and he knew when to get up.

On one occasion Lunch Box heard a bump downstairs but the curtains were still closed, something was not right. He got out of bed and stealthily descended the stairs; nearing the bottom he became aware of a shadow moving around in the living room. As he prepared to open the door and enter the living room, he picked up a Dimple whisky bottle that was used to collect five pence pieces and also served as a door stopper.

As Lunch Box opened the glass panelled door the shadow pulled the door open, our hero swung the bottle and connected with something. The next thing he remembered was waking up in a bed on a hospital ward.

The shadow, who had been in the progress of burgling Lunch Boxes' house, was also in the hospital and he was suffering from a fractured skull. As the burglar was struck with the whisky bottle he had lunged out with a sharpened screwdriver and stabbed Lunch Box causing considerable blood loss.

I heard about the incident for the first time when I heard a group of Chief and Senior Officers debating whether or not they should suspend Lunch Box. It was decided that their hospitalized officer should be suspended and further they thought it appropriate for him to be interviewed to see if there was evidence to support a charge of Assault Causing Grievous Bodily Harm. None of the group I overheard seemed all that bothered about interviewing the burglar. In reality the man with the screwdriver would be interviewed as a matter of course but he did not figure in the ongoing discussion I witnessed.

In recent years there has been a lot of debate about how far someone can go to protect their property and when you can be acting in self-defence. In the latter instance someone would have to retreat or call out before protecting themselves. For a time, it seemed to be touch and go as to whether or not Lunch Box would become a criminal.

For me his actions were quite normal and spontaneous. Who in their right mind would have stopped in bed and shouted, "get out of my house," or, "I'm coming to get you." The Director of Public Prosecutions thought the case should go to court, but on arrival there the jury and the judge found the accused not guilty and common sense had prevailed. Lunch Box returned to work sometime later and worked in the Courts Section until he retired several years later.

At the time that Lunch Box was waiting to go to court the Prison Officers Association decided to 'work to rule'. They did not go out on strike but the industrial action that they did take resulted in a huge strain being put on the capacity of police cells. Some of the cell blocks in police stations were designated as Prison Cells for the duration of the dispute.

For a time, police officers who were drafted in to perform warder duties earned large amounts of overtime money and as usual some became greedy, putting themselves down to work every day off they were supposed to have.

One day an administrative officer came to see me with a claim form submitted by a police sergeant. The policeman had submitted a claim form for the early turn, the late turn and the night shift on the same day. If this was true, he had never gone home and not been off work for twenty-four hours. The rate of pay on rest days was time and a half so one day like that would earn the claimant thirty-six hours pay!

The officer, Paul Smith, who figured in the account of my earlier years as a police officer, was well known to me and I knew the claim would be honest. However, competent as he was, no one should be working a whole day with no sleep at all. His health would be at risk and mistakes would inevitably have been made. When I spoke to him a story of desperation emerged. Some months earlier he had been shopping and tendered his credit card at a department store. To his amazement his card was declined. Confident that his bank balance was healthy he went to the nearest branch. There to his shock he found his account overspent by thousands of pounds. His wife had been on an immense and irresponsible spending spree. They had separated soon after this discovery, but he had agreed to clear the debt.

Never again could he be allowed to work three shifts in one day, but I do know that he cleared the debts in record time. The experience seemed to change him from my point of view. Prior to the discovery he had been a fairly normal steady sort of person but from that point onwards he certainly seemed to develop some eccentric traits. I would best describe him as a 'born again trader'. He became addicted to Ebay and saw bargains as a means to profit. At one stage he had over a dozen vehicles parked in or around the police station. Some he drove, some he intended to work on and sell. He was always 'seeing opportunities.

The police station had a sports and social club which, amongst other things, accumulated a collection of DIY tools and hired them out to members at a reasonable rate. Paul saw a cement mixer at a very reasonable price and the profit lights lit in his eyes. He would purchase it and sell it immediately to the social club. Unfortunately, the sports and social club did not want to buy a cement mixer at the time. For several weeks the mixer stood forlornly on the road outside the station with his car collection until he brought it into the building. There it adorned the sergeants' office for a few more weeks until a Health and Safety inspection reported that it had to be moved out.

Over time the area around his desk became a treasure trove of bric a brac and it was the centre of his trading empire. From Ebay he diversified into dealing in wine, spirits and tobacco products. I once went to his home to pick up a case of Cotes du Rhone wine. The house was clean and basically tidy but there was a full bathroom suite of bath, sink, and toilet in the middle of his living room. All the windows had been stripped of paint and a full facelift was obviously planned.

Over a full year later I again went to his house to get some more wine. To my amazement the bathroom suite still sat in exactly the same place and the windows remained unpainted. He stored his wine in his garage, and it was a real struggle to get into or out of it. I inadvertently put my foot into the grass box of a lawnmower which was partly full of grass clippings, however, there seemed to be something solid under the grass. On inspection, of that which I had put my foot on, I found a dismantled but obviously expensive Fuji camera. Paul had undertaken to fix the camera several months earlier and had completely forgotten he had it.

As the years passed Pauls' house became more and more cluttered and less and less tidy. It greatly resembled 'Steptoe's' yard'. There were undoubtedly some objects of real value among the junk, but I doubt even he knew what was there. His house was not merely full of the items he had purchased but also all the boxes and containers that they had arrived in.

Several years after his twenty-four hour shift he decided to marry again, and the boxes had to go so that his bride could move around the house in her wedding dress. The kitchen was fully refitted after his new wife moved in but some of the cupboards and drawers did not survive long. Paul put a car battery on the work surface and attached it to a battery charger. The battery leaked, corroded the work surface and eventually fell through into the cupboard beneath. The acid fully leaked out destroying more shelves and drawers. Husband and wife just worked round the mess and left the battery where it had come to rest.

Another purchase was a large marquee type tent which was supposed to provide cover at a party in his garden. It arrived in a Furniture Removal van and with friends and neighbours they struggled to get it through the house into the rear lawned area. Only when the tent arrived at its destination did everyone realise it was far too big for the garden. Weeks became months and months became years until the tent eventually became overgrown with grass and weeds. It is probably still there.

Pauls' wife was surprised one day when a gentleman arrived to view a car that our trader was selling. Clearly unaware of a car she rang Paul who told her that the car in question was in the garage! The couple had been married for several years by this stage and to the best of her knowledge the garage was full of the boxes that had been moved out to make way for her wedding dress. The prospective purchaser and the wife set about moving empty boxes out of the garage and an hour later they revealed a Porsche that Mrs. Smith had not even known about.

I would say that Pauls' ventures were to say the least mercurial. He saw an opportunity in the holiday business when he heard that some flight companies only operated between certain dates and sometimes the last flight back from a resort was always nearly empty. Paul researched flights and found one that fitted the bill. The problem was getting people to the resort by another means.

After considerable effort Paul came up with the idea of hiring a coach for the outward journey to the Costa Brava. This would be followed by five nights in the resort and then there would be the flight back. Tickets were sold through the Sports and Social Club (who provided a further discount) and the holiday was soon sold out. I have heard that everyone who went enjoyed themselves, but I do not believe that the venture was particularly profitable, and it was not repeated the following year.

A later venture into the holiday trade was on a much smaller scale. He decided he would take his wife touring and to do that he needed a caravan. Ebay was perused yet again, and he quickly identified a low budget purchase. He bought what had once been a fast-food trailer, selling burgers, hot dogs and chips from lay byes at the side of the road. After considerable work the cooking equipment was removed, and he was left with what was effectively an empty box on a trailer. It still had the serving hatch, and the original paint scheme still identified it as 'Billys' Burgers'.

In the space where the chip fryer and griddle had been Paul lay two duck feather sleeping bags. All systems were go, though the journey from Yorkshire to Scotland took far longer than had been anticipated. Arriving late at night, on the shores of Loch Ness, they fell asleep to the lapping of water after consuming a bottle of vodka.

The following morning, they were still almost comatose after the long journey. Suddenly there was a loud banging at the side of the trailer. Paul could not get to the side of the trailer because of his wife's body in her sleeping bag so he opened the hatch. Looking out he saw a small boy standing on tiptoes to look in.

"Can I have two burgers and some chips Mr.?" Asked the boy.

I am sure the youngster went away after a pleasant exchange with our holidaymaker.

It would be possible to go on and on with stories about Paul who became something of a legend in our Force. However, in drawing this snapshot to a close I cannot but mention one last incident. Paul lived on the same street as I did, and you can imagine the state of the house from what I have already told you. One day a friend came to see me and said that he had just visited Pauls to check the house while he was away on holiday. The friend thought that the house had been burgled but he wasn't certain if the mess was just as it always had been. Sadly, on this occasion some of the destruction had been caused by intruders. We discovered later that lots of items had been stolen but months later the insurance company had not paid out as Paul could not say exactly what had been taken. The Loss Adjustor could not believe that anything of value had been taken from the chaotic mess in the house and in the end, Paul gave up on the claim as it would have been too difficult to tidy up.

Finally, it seems from the stories I have told that Paul must have lacked the basic organization and reliability to be a police officer. I must put that record straight. Although his appearance, speech and lifestyle caused his supervisors great concern he achieved considerable results in any job that he was given. In the final years of his career Paul became an inspector and made his area a much safer place to live, though to the end he was upsetting senior officers including my deputy, who on an inspection saw that Paul had orange bale twine fastening his boots instead of laces.

This has been just a sample of the characters who were around at this stage of my career. There will be more later, but for now I must return to the sequence of events.

CHAPTER SEVEN

THE SECTOR

Becoming a sector commander was strange. It required a whole different approach. The sub division had had one hundred and twenty officers covering a geographical area some thirty miles in length and ten miles in width. The sector had twenty officers and covered four miles by two miles. With the sub division you were dealing with broad brush strokes and leaving others to fill in the detail. On a sector you had to focus on the small detail if you wanted to achieve results.

Any sector commander would have to work out who the 'doers' and 'movers' in the local community were. For me the Town Council was a good place to start. I had attended the Council Meetings as deputy Sub Divisional Commander and the business usually followed a set format. I read out the crime figures and detection rates and then commented on any events that were taking place. The Chair would thank me and then councillors and members of the public were given the chance to air their own problems and concerns.

The public could be quite hostile but very often they wanted to discuss national issues which I could do little about and generally the discussion veered from issue to issue like a runaway train. After about twenty minutes the Chair would say that the meeting had to move on to the next agenda item and I was released. The next meeting would follow exactly the same format and I am sure that everyone regarded the policing item as window dressing rather than outcome based.

I decided to invite the councillors to the police station to discuss what we could really do to solve the many issues raised by their constituents. Reluctantly, the majority of them did turn up. I stressed that the police did not have a magic wand to put all societys' problems right but that if we truly had a bash at working out what the problems really were then we, or someone, could do something.

Amazingly, at that first meeting two councillors, who represented the residents of a large council estate, could only come up with dog fouling as a problem. I had to respond in a vaguely negative way saying that the police usually did not know whose dogs were the ones leaving the mess.

At the next meeting the same councillors again raised the issue of dog dirt. They had asked for an easel and a board which we managed to provide. When the meeting started the board was covered in a blanket and it remained there like a symbol of doom until we were well into the meeting. Then the councillors asked to present their evidence and approached the easel. With a flourish the blanket was swept away from the board and there was a huge, glossy, black and white photograph of one street on their council estate. White circles had been superimposed on the photograph using what looked like Tip X (which for those unfamiliar with typing, prior to computers, this was used to make corrections on completed work). On closer inspection there was a darker object in the centre of each white circle and at the side of them was a number, also in white. The councillors explained that each circle surrounded a pile of dog dirt, and the number identified the house that the offending dog belonged to.

They must have spent hours watching the street and a not insubstantial cost in preparing the photograph. I assured them that we would make use of the evidence before the next meeting, but the question remained very much how and what we could do? Clearly the councillors would not give statements against the offending owners as many of the offenders would have voted for them. There had to be another way.

I was usually dealing with the Town Council, but this time decided to contact the County Council and ask them what involvement they had with dog dirt issues. They were interested and wanted to meet. Dog fouling was a major issue for them, they too were inundated with letters of complaint, and they agreed to host the meeting.

I was surprised that the meeting was organized so quickly and amazed to find that the Chair was the Chief Executive of the Council. That get together had a momentous impact on my sector. I left the meeting with contact details for the Housing Department, Street Cleansing, the Dog Warden service and the Legal Services Department.

All the contacts that I subsequently visited were like a breath of fresh air. Just coming together gave us ideas on how to tackle the problem because we all saw the same issue in a slightly different way. It helped establish a format for tackling all problems where outcomes could not be achieved by a single agency.

My team leafletted the area worst affected by dog fouling. We informed the residents of the size of the fines, the civil liability that dog owners had if their animal caused a nuisance or bit someone. It was also pointed out that if their dog caused a traffic accident then the owner could end up paying compensation. The Housing Department sent out letters reminding Council tenants that they could be evicted if they caused nuisance in their areas and, further, their dogs could be regarded as a nuisance for this purpose. Street cleaning officers did a high-profile street clean and fitted bins and signs. Finally, dog wardens targeted the area and took dogs without collars and identification tags into their pounds, owners of the animals had to pay to get them back.

Slowly and surely, what had been called 'Shit Alley' had been cleaned up. The local newspaper ran a positive story. It had all seemed obvious but in the past suspicion, jealousy and stereotyping had prevented agencies working together properly. This was a positive result, and the timing was perfect.

All this happened at the same time that Problem Solving Policing was being discussed at the Police Staff College. I cannot claim to have been tuned into the new initiative when I lumbered into using its' techniques. Problem Solving was based on a programme called 'Broken Windows' from New York. The basis of the approach was that as areas started to deteriorate people lost respect for their environment and themselves. Broken windows led to graffiti, led to criminal damage, led to property crime and the development of a generally anti-social neighbourhood. Fix the windows, clean the graffiti off, sweep the streets and the areas started to pick up and crime dropped.

In New York there are umpteen types of police. There are transport police, parks police, Shopping Malls police, you name it there was a police force for it. Before the introduction of the 'Broken Windows' programme none of the police spoke to each other, just as the agencies avoided each other in my area. When the police groups began to reach out to each other they realized that their combined strength could be phenomenal.

Now a few paragraphs ago you may have been thinking, "I could have read a book about an explorer, or a pop star or a sportsman, and this guy wants to write about dog shit!" However, you are now on the edge of discovering the secret that, for a while, made policing work as it was designed to. Decide what is the cause of the problem, then target all the available resources at removing the cause. Years later Tony Blairs' New Labour would have a slogan. "Tough on Crime. Tough on the Causes of Crime." My team and our allies had it working before the method was a twinkling in Tonys' eyes.

One problem we faced with policing the large council estate on the sector was that we had only two cars and it was a thirty-minute walk from the station to the estate. There were two officers allocated to the estate, so we lost forty hours a month just having them walking to and from their beat once a day. This wasted time was the equivalent of an extra officer on the beat and I quoted that at one of the councillor meetings which were now attended by all the agencies.

The Housing Department of the County Council came up with the goods. In those days there was no shortage of public housing in our area. Indeed, very few wanted to live on our Council estate. There were numerous boarded up houses which were euphemistically called 'voids'. The Housing representative saw no problem in one of them being let to the police and we snapped their hand off. The house was identified, secured and alarmed, the officers decorated the house in their own time, and we moved in desks, lockers and kitchen facilities soon afterwards. There was a grand public opening which attracted even more positive publicity.

For a year everything went well. Crime and the number of reports of anti-social behaviour fell dramatically. Some councillors stopped coming to the 'multi agency' meeting because they thought we had succeeded and the officers working on the estate were able to spend more time providing inputs at the schools, fetes etc. Sadly, there were problems ahead.

Social Services were looking for a drop-in centre for women who had been victims of domestic violence. The first floor of the building we occupied was little used. There was an opportunity, they asked, I agreed and the drop in was up and running within days. Unfortunately, some women who had been abused did not want to attend a building where police worked. I can fully understand where the victims were coming from, and I should have seen that there would be problems. Some of the victims would already have been let down by the police, some will have been pressurised into giving evidence against their partners and, worse, some of them will have become repeat victims because they had involved the police previously.

Fourteen months after the house was opened for police use, we withdrew. We were the victims of our success. The neighbourhood had improved dramatically so other problems needed resolving and the victims of domestic violence probably needed the house more than us.

One other major achievement while we used the house was to help improve things at the secondary school. Things were bad there. Exam results were terrible, truancy levels were high, and the school was regularly vandalized, frequently burgled and the playing fields were used by car thieves to race and then burn out the vehicles they had acquired.

There had been little attention paid to crime prevention measures and we quickly put a lot of those into place. There was anti vandal paint, no climb features, bars on vulnerable windows, sensor lights and most successful of all the entrances were gated or bollarded (cars could no longer get in or out when the school was closed). All this seems basic nowadays, but it had big results in those days. A visitor from the Home Office came soon after our initiatives started to be noticed and he said to me, "Ah! I see you've been picking the low hanging fruit." I knew exactly what he meant but I did not share the put down with my team.

In spite of all the 'fruit harvesting' there were still break ins and vandalism, so we decided to spend a few night shifts in the school. After a week of doing this with regular officers I decided to give Special Constables a chance (Specials are volunteers who are given basic training and issued with uniforms...often referred to as 'Hobby Bobbies' some of them were absolutely fantastic and totally dedicated.)

Nowadays health and safety regulations have ensured that 'Specials' would not be allowed to perform observation duties on their own. However, ours performed the 'obs' well. One night as they kept watch they heard the distinctive sound of wood splintering and they rushed to where the noise was coming from. They ended up facing two would be burglars through a doors glass window. I am uncertain who was the most shocked, it seems that on both sides of the door everyone froze. The Specials could not get out and the burglars could not get in, it was a stand-off. Eventually the 'baddies' decided to run away and shortly thereafter the Specials, having worked out how to get out, had chased them, but there were no prisoners that night.

The following night the Specials turned out in force again. After a short time of watching, they detected activity in one of the doorways. They could not see what was happening as it was pitch black outside. This time they had mastered the opening of the security doors from the inside. As the doors swung open our team were given a close-up view of a young couple engaged in frantic sexual activity on the floor of the doorway.

Following the period of intensive observations crime attacks on the school dropped. I suppose part of the success was simply down to the fact that the message, we were there, got out to the criminal fraternity and they went off to easier targets. Our efforts at the school took on a softer dimension with police officers giving lessons and attending fetes and social events in the grounds. We even played a couple of cricket matches against pupils and parents. To me it seemed that a community spirit seemed to be emerging though perhaps it had always been there and had been forced underground by anti-social behaviour. In any event I felt we were making a difference.

We started to get interest from outside the Force and one day I had a phone call from a local Member of Parliament who wanted to come and have a look at what we were doing. The man came early in the morning and remained all day listening carefully to everything that was said to him. At the end of his visit the MP said that he would be writing to the Chief Constable praising what we were doing and suggesting that the whole Force adopt our methods. Further, there was a vague suggestion that my team should receive some sort of award or recognition because of their efforts. Then we heard nothing for what seemed like a long time, and I assumed the visit had just been 'window dressing and hot air'.

It was out of the blue when I was called to Headquarters. I was not informed why I had been summoned but when I arrived, I was called to see the new Chiefs' Staff Officer. We were of the same rank and yet I felt like I was being given a telling off. I was informed that the Chief was not happy with me and was particularly annoyed that I had spoken to the MP before briefing him. Further, the Chief was annoyed that the publicity given to my initiative would detract from a strategy that he had just launched.

Now, I have already indicated that my relationship with the Chief was, to say the least, strained but this was a further step on the way to no return. The Chiefs' new strategy was called 'Quality of Life Policing.' For the life of me I could not see what I had done that could detract from that. I had submitted reports to Chief Officers about what we were doing and the Chief would, I believe, have got the credit for introducing sectors. Quality of Life was for me, however, the biggest waste of time, money and effort that I had yet seen in policing.

The new strategy was about speaking nicely to people, opening more reception desks at police stations, sending letters to victims of crime and 'cleaning up' the CID. None of those strands had anything to do with the problem-solving approach that we were applying on an everyday basis. The strategy was cosmetic, we were making a real difference in a community. I said all this to the Staff Officer on the basis I was talking to a receptive peer, but I should have known better.

A year later one of the community leaders from my sector asked if I had got the 'honour' yet. I did not know what he meant. Certainly, I was able to inform him that the last comment to me had been a critical, one akin to a slap in the face. Subsequently I found that, at the MP's suggestion, I had been nominated for a Queens' Police Medal. A comprehensive file had been put together with evidence and inputs from all sorts of people. The papers had gone as far as the Chief and there it had stopped. My Force rarely put nominations through, but the award was supposed to be given to those who still had enough service left to enjoy having it. The few that were put through from our Force were usually Chief Officers. On the event of my one and only nomination the Chief did put someone forward and to the amazement of the Force it went to the platinum blond assistant who had accompanied the Chief during the eastern bloc escapade. If that was what you got it for, I did not want it. I had decided to stay out of the Chiefs' way by now. My career had stalled big time but whatever he thought of me, I knew what I thought of him. I was enjoying myself doing something that made a difference.

CHAPTER EIGHT

STILL AT THE SECTOR

After the first few months on the sector, I regarded all the team as personal friends. I genuinely believe that rank was not an issue, we all worked on first name terms even if that had been frowned upon by the powers that be. We had a log of things that needed to be done and everyone updated the log each day, endorsing what they had done, added new things or asked for someone else to help out. Some of the town councillors even called into the station and recorded what they had done or needed to be done. It worked!

I was regularly contacted by people who had known me when I was deputy sub divisional commander of the much bigger area. It always seemed hard to refer them to others if they were not based on or living in the sector. One character I knew well ran a large Burger restaurant called 'Alabama Burger'. It was an impressive place with a massive pink American Cadillac on the roof. The walls were decorated with original memorabilia and the eating area felt to be an authentic USA experience. The owner was a small man, quite effeminate in his mannerisms with a brushed over hairstyle and his glasses hung from a gold chain. At times he could be abrupt and rude with a ferocious attitude towards children. However, the food was excellent, and people flocked there in their droves.

On one occasion the owner turned up at the Town Council Meeting and initially he would not speak to me. When we came to the section of the meeting that covered 'any other business' he jumped to his feet.

"I wish to complain that the Police have changed their phone number so that I cannot ring in!"

The Chair peered at him and then at me.

"Do you know anything about the telephone numbers changing?" I was asked.

"I know of no telephone changes. Ours are just the same as they have been for months."

"Well," exploded the restaurateur. "I've been ringing you every few hours and every time I get a fucking Chinese Take Away!"

Only then did it start to sink in. The owner had been ringing me on the number I had used when I was deputy sub divisional commander. My old office was now occupied by a Chinese man who was an officer from the Hong Kong Police Force, seconded to our Force for experience as a superintendent. I explained this to the meeting.

"That may be alright for Crispy Fucking Duck." Said the man. "But I want a real police officer."

He then smiled and sat down. I gave him my new number and he would ring at all times of day asking me for Chicken with Hoi Sin sauce before telling me what he really wanted. He still rang me years later when I was by then a Divisional Commander in a totally different area, he just needed his own contact!

I think it was on a visit to the 'Alabama' that I first heard of 'Raves'. At that time those events were becoming a phenomenon across the whole country and were beset with policing problems. People, eager for a quick financial gain, identified a derelict or empty building, broke in or got a short-term lease and then arranged events with loud disco music that went on all night.

The whole point of Raves was that they were organized quickly, advertised covertly, held for one night and then everyone moved to another venue often miles away. There was no chance for any safety inspections, the grant or consideration of licensing and no chance of anyone paying taxes. Thus, events were held in buildings that were structurally unsound, lacking in water, toilets and refreshments. Electric was often supplied by generators with no fall-back power if those machines failed.

One or two of these events had been held outside with thousands of people in attendance. Policing them was a nightmare, even if we knew about them it was often too late to stop them. If we did know about them, we either had to send large numbers of police officers or turn a blind eye to the event and hope the night would pass safely.

The owner of Alabama informed me that he had heard of a local businessman who was looking for a suitable building to hold a rave in our area. I tasked my staff to have a look and see if they could identify any likely premises. I was very worried and did not want to play at ostriches as the Force seemed most often to do. If the building collapsed, the power failed and people panicked, or impure drugs killed anyone at an event then I knew where the blame would settle.

Within a week of the first hint that planning was afoot, the manager of the Cargo Transport Centre rang me. The Cargo Centre was a huge one storey building of concrete blocks and corrugated metal sheeting. It had been used for conferences, auctions and sales but most usually its purpose was for the storage of freight containers. The manager, Bridget Green, was employed to ensure the Centre operated at a profit and she had been offered good money to host a Rave event. She was keen to meet with the organisers but was equally concerned not to break any laws.

I visited the Centre and had a look round; we then discussed the proposal. The premises already had a liquor licence and a music licence; there could be few Health and Safety issues in this vast open space and the Fire Service would dream about the number of easily accessed exits. The Cargo Centre was in a business area and there was no residential accommodation within half a mile. There was abundant car parking, and the other businesses would be closed at night. The more we discussed it, the more I began to think that it could happen. The alternative could be a warehouse without power and with rotten floorboards and we would have no input in something like that. I asked about the identity of the organisers and the manager arranged for us to meet.

There were two men involved in the proposed venture and I must admit that I liked them. They were both local businessmen and if the event backfired, they would have to live with the fallout and there would be an impact on their other ventures. They seemed willing to spend money to make the Rave a success. They had already contacted a well-known security company who usually specialized in large sporting events. The men said that they had considered hiring an ambulance to be on standby at the event and, in for a penny in for a pound, I asked if they would contribute to the extra policing costs, and I was surprised when they said they would.

The organisers and I arranged to meet again, and in the meantime, I spoke to the inspector of the Force Drug Squad who was keen to be involved. The Special Constables all wanted to work at the event, and it was clear that the impetus was growing.

The men came to meet me in the police station for our second get together. They were looking at a crowd of between two and three thousand. The event would start at midnight and run through until dawn. I had insisted on a ticket only basis and they had arranged four ticket outlets which would be carefully monitored, and sales would stop twenty-four hours before doors opened. I asked for the names of all the security staff who were to work on the night, and I wanted them in time to run our own checks on them.

In relation to drugs issues, we agreed that large bins would be placed next to the entrance where those carrying illicit substances had the chance to get rid of them. Security officers would search those attending and a police officer would be present at the point of search. A Police Dog Handler and a dog trained to locate drugs were to be on duty near the entrance and this facility was to be paid for by the organisers. Finally, I asked that the wages of four police officers working outside the venue were to be paid by the organisers and to my amazement they agreed.

My officers and I worked on an 'Operational Plan' which we believed covered all eventualities. However, in spite of all the positive vibes that emanated from the event, I was beginning to feel apprehensive about what I had walked into. I was the most senior officer involved in this and there was no doubt where the buck would stop if things went wrong. One or two things occurred which fed my growing anxiety; firstly, the list of security staff contained several individuals who had unspent convictions and there were three who been imprisoned for murder or manslaughter; secondly, eight hours before the event, we did not know how many were coming. It was also clear that it was now too late to stop the event without a massive police turnout.

The point of no return had been reached and we were as well prepared as we could be. The Drug Squad had placed a 'portacabin' on top of a freight container and they placed staff in there with night glasses and binoculars to view those attending. Uniform officers were highly visible on the approach to the Centre, the security staff were in uniform and looked quite formidable. The premises looked safe inside and out but still I worried.

I expected the noise would impact on our radio communication system even outside the building. However, it was strangely quiet as the event started. The metal panels on the Centre were vibrating but you could hear next to nothing. Then we started to get complaints from locations up to five miles away. I had not considered the way in which sound waves travel and when I went home three hours after the start, I could hear the bass beat in my bedroom a good two miles away from the Centre.

Over two thousand turned up on the night, they came in good spirits and left exhausted some five or six hours after they had arrived. There was a fair quantity of recreational drugs deposited in the bins near the entrance and obviously some will have taken them before entering the premises. There were, however, no reports of any medical issues and the Drugs Squad had sighted no major dealers in the vicinity. Off duty police officers had attended the event socially and said that the whole thing had been run professionally. The organisers had provided a 'Chill Room' where dancers could go to cool down and rest. The only complaints from those attending was the price of bottled water which retailed at ten times the price it would have been in a supermarket. I mentioned this to the organisers, and they asked how much I would pay for an ice cream at a cinema, and they had a point, but there was something more sinister than the price. Someone, probably at the organisers request, had turned off the water in the toilets and this was certainly a health and safety issue even if the intention had been a purely commercial decision.

For days afterwards my staff felt a 'buzz' at how well the event had gone off. To the best of our knowledge, we had been the first to cooperate with the organization of a Rave. My elation lasted only two days. I received a phone call from the Chiefs' Office and the conversation went something like this.

"The Chief understands that you are proposing to support an illegal Rave event and he does not want us to be involved."

I explained that the event had now taken place and had gone off successfully.

"The Chief will ask why he did not know about this."

" Well, the Chief should ask my Divisional Commander because he had a copy of the Operational Order."

There was a pause and then,

"The Chief does not want you commanding any more such events, you're not senior enough in rank. No more."

That was it. No thank you, or congratulations. I just wanted to point out that in a few days I would be commanding a big rugby league match with over ten thousand attending but that would be OK because no one else wanted to work on a Sunday. I was the only person in the country who had commanded an event such as that and yet again I was sidelined. However, the feeling did not last long because the rugby match, unusually, exploded into a public disorder fiesta. Spectators threw things at each other, fans were urinating in the stand, one of the players abused a police officer and some cars were damaged when the match ended. All that was a normal event, and no one bothered to say I should not command the next one!

I never did control another Rave and I was never used in any training provided to officers who did. Was I bothered? Probably, on balance, not. Because I could be pragmatic about it. You never knew if one slightly different occurrence were to happen then an event can go badly wrong. The death of a teenager who has taken drugs, a fire in the premises, a fight/knifing, any of those things and the nine till five brigade would be out in force working out who to blame. I had done my event and got away with it.......

CHAPTER NINE

THE STALEMATE BREAKS

As time ticked by, I suddenly realized that I had not seen the Chief in over a year and when I contemplated this fact, I realized I was quite happy by it. To be honest I cannot remember who my Divisional Commander was at that time, so the 'big guns' were leaving me alone, it was as if I did not exist. Yet the downside of being ignored was that I could end up retiring from the sector without having tried anything else. It was eleven years since I had returned from the Special Course and some of my contemporaries from that time were already Assistant Chief Constables. Somewhere in the depths of my psyche lurked a bit of competitiveness and a splash of ambition.

There was very little I could do about progressing my career. The Chief had made it clear that he did not recognize the Chief Inspector rank, even though other Forces did. There were several of us stuck in this limbo land but there seemed to be no way out. I could apply for a vacancy in another Force hoping that I would get a good testimonial, or I could complain to the HMI (Her Majesty's Inspector of Constabulary.) during an inspection and, if that failed, I would be in an even worse position.

I had never seen anyone win a battle against a serving Chief Constable and I really did not want to move from the Force I was serving in. Then, two things happened in quick succession.

Firstly, I saw a Home Office vacancy advertised in the Police Review (a professional journal for police officers). A Chief Inspector was wanted to coordinate the Graduate Entry Scheme. The post holder would have a flat in London but would then travel throughout England and Wales, visiting Universities and Colleges in order to attract graduates to the Police Service.

The job appealed to me, and I filled in an application form. After a short time, I received an invitation to the Home Office to take part in a day long interview process. As days passed, I started to have doubts about pursuing the job, but I waited until it was too late to pull out. On the day of the interview, I got up at five o' clock in the morning and caught the first train to Kings Cross. I had no idea what sort of things the interview process would cover but spent most of the journey reading the sports pages of the morning's newspapers.

Arriving in London, a little after nine, plunged me into a seething maelstrom of humanity. Everyone seemed to be rushing, all with a purpose like worker ants but determined not to make eye contact with anyone else. The noise was horrendous, and I admit that it was disorienting for someone who was a country boy at heart.

I had no idea how to get to the Home Office and I was reluctant to plunge into the Underground. After a few minutes I saw a man standing and looking into the window of a Boots Chemists store, he looked vaguely familiar. He was the only person not dashing to get somewhere so I approached him. The result of the meeting was somehow surreal.

"Excuse me. Could you tell me the way to the Home Office." I asked.

The man turned from the window and as he did, so I recognized him as Gerald Kaufman the Labour MP. He looked me up and down and then said.

"I've been trying to get there for years, but geographically it is not all that far."

He gave me a detailed route of how to get to the Home Office and I arrived in plenty of time for the interview. I felt that although I clearly did not like being in London seeing Gerald Kauffman had been a sort of omen. I felt fairly upbeat when I arrived at the Government Building and negotiated the security without any problem.

There were ten of us to go through the selection process and as we sat together in a waiting room, I was less than impressed with most of the candidates. A teacher once said to me that a teacher would take several weeks to get to know a pupil, but a pupil would judge a teacher in the first few minutes. Well, I had that bunch assessed within record time. Most of them fell into the bumptious, arrogant, egotistical category and sitting with them made me feel a little nauseous.

The rest of the day was in many ways a blur. There were a number of interviews and some written work, then at lunchtime I went for a walk among the bustle, noise and fumes. While wandering I decided that this really was not for me. Don't get me wrong, a trip to London to visit a museum, see a show or attend a sports fixture and everything would be fine, but strip the window dressing and London was not for me.

Early in the afternoon some of the applicants were thanked but told that they could leave as they had been unsuccessful. Five of us remained and by mid-afternoon we had been whittled down to three. There was one more interview and the decision would be announced. I definitely did not want this job and had to find a way of not getting it. The answer was to make a mess of the last interview and rely on the other two to perform well.

Three Chief Officers sat behind a desk as I faced them. The Chair of the panel was a large, grey-haired female. She looked at me, screwed her face up as if she was going to ask me the most difficult question in the world and she said,

"Where do you see the role of Neighbourhood Police Officers in the modern Police Service.?"

I could not believe she had just asked me a question about my pet subject. It was like the final question in 'Who wants to be a Millionaire?' and they ask something you know the answer to. This was a gift. I had had my greatest success with Local Policing Teams, and I was a believer in them. For me, targeted neighbourhood policing teams were the answer, and I was off. Then slowly I realized that the Chief Officers were sitting forward and smiling, and I realised that I was talking myself into a life in London. I managed to start talking about CID crime teams, the growth in cyber-crime (which at the time I knew nothing about) and said there would be no place for neighbourhood policing. I felt like a traitor to my team at home and to my own beliefs. What a load of twaddle I gave them, but they thanked me profusely at the end of the interview.

We were called back one at a time and I was told that I had come second. The feedback was that I had been a long way ahead at lunchtime but had faded badly in the afternoon. Thank goodness for the escape strategy! I relaxed for the first time that day as the train travelled north. All I wanted was to take the dog for a walk and have a pint in my local pub. However, the end was neither tidy nor final.

The following morning, I received a phone call informing me that the chosen candidate had withdrawn, and they were inviting me to take the post. If one of the Chief Officers had rung me, I would have been too embarrassed to say no, but the call came from a staff officer. So, I told him that I didn't want the job either as I didn't like to be second choice. My Force had already been told I was to be given the job and they had committed the posting to paper. I received formal notification from the Chief when I had already said no!

Fortunately, the person who came third was keen to take the post. I was staying where I was. I wondered if all this had caused a ripple in the Forces' corridors of power. It is probable that there was not even a blink as the Chief walked blindly towards a major personnel crisis. There had been no promotion to a senior post for over three years and the impact on morale was extremely negative.

Suddenly the Home Office undermined our Chiefs' cost cutting strategy by rejecting some of the proposals of the Sheehy Report. Chief Inspector was to remain a valuable rank in managerial progression. Over the period of time when my Force froze promotion other Forces continued to promote while waiting for a final decision from Government. All of us who had been Chief Inspectors when the freeze was applied had had our careers suspended. I had been on course but now looked up at people from my Special Course who were Assistant Chief Constables. However, I could at least celebrate the fact that my rank was recognized again. I was a Chief Inspector!

The Chief Constable decided that he would hold Assessment Centres to create a list from whom he would promote as vacancies arose. There had never been any structure to the method of appointing senior officers in our Force. Promotion was a matter of the Chief deciding who he wanted and that was it. These new 'tests' seemed very strange, and we were all a little apprehensive. The overall feeling was that anything was better from what had been going on.

CHAPTER TEN

ASSESSMENTS

Assessment Centres became a monster of their own creation. They should not have been needed because the Annual Performance Appraisals should have provided all the information that the Chief Constable needed. Sadly, those appraisals were treated as 'happy sheets'. I think some managers would not, or could not, be objective about their staff.

Some dire and useless 'uniform carriers' received appraisals that described them as "competent, professional and achieving the required standard." The appraisal process was a time-consuming waste of effort because everyone met the required standard unless a supervisor didn't like someone.

It was incompetence that made Assessment Centres necessary. However, there was still the big question of which officers would be allowed to attend the centres. How did the service decide who they were; they decided to use the appraisal system! Therefore, where was the evidence that could prevent the 'useless' from attending the Assessment Centres.

In the early years those who were not that good as police officers did not do too well in the assessment process. Then the monster grew. There was a demand for trained assessors, and they were selected from the ranks of the Police Service. The training for the assessors focused on how to look for evidence of skills in responses to questions, how to record the evidence and how to mark the replies. Those who had been trained as assessors would at a future date attend an Assessment Centre and there, surprise, surprise, they did very well in playing the evidence game.

Advice on how to do well in the centres was passed on and there were arranged practice sessions and 'dummy runs.' It became possible to pass by focusing on the skills required for the rank and preparing evidence of those skills even before the centres took place. The 'evidence' did not have to be based on anything the candidates had actually done and some of it was completely fabricated. It became a matter of learning the techniques and playing the game.

Years later, I had a superintendent working for me who spent hours practicing the answers for 'Psychometric Tests.' Those tests were designed to evidence traits when candidates were asked a huge number of written questions in a short period of time. If someone became really good at the tests, they could identify the traits that were being looked for and respond according to what the job was looking for. The techniques required for the different sections of the 'Centres' became a cottage industry and at times had more effort focused on them than on the Law.

The Police Service is now managed by officers who have been cloned. You can see or hear them being interviewed by the media and you will never get a feel of real emotion or originality, they are just speaking on auto pilot as if they were undergoing an Assessment Centre. Real people get things wrong every now and then but at least they do have feelings and can display a warm open-hearted response to a tragedy.

The Police Service is now sanitized and politically correct. Chief Officers are never heard of now because they are never controversial until, that is, they get their tits out in a bar or have been caught fiddling their expenses. Some are, I am sure, people with opinions and may be good managers---but wouldn't it be good to hear their views not to be bombarded with saccharin platitudes?

Now, I must return to the Assessment Centre I was submitted to. I attended after several years as a Chief Inspector. There were well over twenty candidates and some of those were Inspectors who were allowed to participate.

The event was held in the Force Training Centre, a three-storey building, shoe box shaped and constructed out of concrete and glass. It was planned to be performed on a Saturday when assessors from other Forces could attend to assist ours.

There were five components to the day. These consisted of an interview, a letter writing exercise, a presentation, a media test and a written problem solving. It would be an intense day and for most of us it would be a first experience.

For me the day started well, or at least it felt like it had and by lunchtime I had had an interview, completed the letter writing and had overcome the presentation. The last of those components had been the most testing as one of the assessors was very well known to me. We had discussed police matters regularly and we were both clear where we stood. Here I had to tow the party line and just hope that he marked from that.

The lunch break was as fraught as the tests had been, with people comparing answers and stating how they had felt at each stage. The nervous energy expended was incredible and I already felt exhausted. In the afternoon I actually enjoyed the Problem Solving; from recollection, it was not a police problem and revolved around where to place a new road. I now had forty minutes before my media test and took myself to the canteen for a coffee.

I had recently completed a media course at the Police Staff College, and I had been told that I had performed well at that. I was actually looking forward to the final exercise until the Chief arrived and threw my day into chaos and confusion. I was told that the Chief wanted to interview me in a one to one. This had not appeared on the days schedule and only two of us had been selected for the extra interview. The explanation for being subjected to the Chiefs' input was that he wanted to exercise a quality control of the event by having an input.

My interview went on for nearly an hour after the exercises had been running for five hours already. He had set questions but asked regular subsidiary questions. I did not like the man and to me it was a battle of getting through without being brow beaten into making mistakes. When it eventually ended, I felt like I could not get out of the chair. The interview room was on the top floor of the building, and I was not certain if my legs would support me as I waited to descend. I was also late for the media exercise. I cannot remember anything about the last exercise, and I was just pleased to get home.

Then there was the waiting, which dragged on as week after week slipped by. None of us could understand the delay as the exercises were marked then and there. My overwhelming feeling was that I had not been treated fairly. How can an hour-long interview with the most powerful man in the Force not have an impact on the exercise that came afterwards. When the results did eventually emerge the media test had been my weakest score. With a steady performance in that last half hour, I could well have come first yet, as it was, I came fourth.

Most importantly for everyone was how long the list would be of those who had been successful. If they only wanted three, then I was out thanks to the Chief. After more waiting it was announced that the list was to be eight. I was in, the pain had been worthwhile.

The Chief was to remain in office for another three or four years and things did not get any better in Force. It did seem that what had been a personal dislike of me receded. Although I felt uncomfortable around him there were no real confrontations in spite of the fact, we attended some of the same meetings. I think it only fair and relevant to pass a few comments on his legacy to the Force here.

No two people will share exactly the same view about a third person. Further, the way this Chief treat me would hardly result in my singing his praises. However, I am sure that some will have been impressed by him. Indeed, one person who did hold him in high regard was one of our local MP's. That individual was fairly well qualified to comment as he had also been the Chair of the Force Police Authority and I had a lot of time for him on the basis of the huge amount of constituency work he did.

Years after the Chiefs' departure the MP sung his praises during the meeting of a Parliamentary Working Group. His comments were based on the fact that the Chief had attempted to stop police officers visiting criminals in prison. Some of you may wonder what that was all about.

Imagine Billy the Burglar caught red handed climbing out of a window with a bag of 'swag'. He is interviewed, admits the offence (or not) and goes to court where he is convicted, sentenced and sent to prison. There Billy gets fairly bored, looks forward to getting his visits and gets on with doing his 'time'.

Now, while Billy festers the Police are worried by the rise in the frequency of burglary and the fall in the Forces' detection rate. They peruse the whole pile of undetected burglary reports, and they find a number that were committed using a similar method to that which Billy employed. The Police decide to go and talk to Billy, they take him some cigarettes and sweets. They tell him that if he 'clears his slate' he will not be bothered on his release. "Ah!" says Billy. "If I admit a load of jobs, will they increase my sentence?" He is immediately assured that there will be no punishment attached to his admissions, the whole job is purely for administrative purposes and no downside for him.

Billy willingly admits to twenty or thirty other 'jobs' which he may or may not have done and everyone is happy. At that time, it was assumed that the public would be assured when they saw detection rates of fifty percent plus and were satisfied that lots of burglars were held to account for their actions. But the whole process could be a little dubious. Some Forces would take Billy out of Prison and let him show them where he had committed his crimes, but some unscrupulous detectives just accepted Billy's word for what he had done.

If you looked carefully at the offences Billy had admitted, you may well find some that had been performed by miraculous means. Especially as he had been in custody when the offence took place. The crime figures at that time were unreliable as they were massaged and manipulated. The whole process was shady, and peoples' careers were made by cheating.

Now our Chief wanted the Force to be ethical and there can be little argument with that. In consequence visits to prisons were all but banned. The detection rate fell alarmingly, and the Detective Chief Superintendent was removed from his post and replaced by an officer with little CID experience and a remit to clean up the dodgy practices.

The CID became 'persona non grata' overnight, morale fell, and many looked for jobs away from crime fighting. It all looks good on the face of it, but the reality was that the great majority of CID officers were hard working, honest police officers. They worked hours of unpaid overtime; they followed procedures that had always been followed and now they were condemned for doing what they had been told to do.

The flaw in all this was the way that the change was managed. An initial approach might have been to tighten up the matching of an admission with a crime. Certainly, some Forces did do exactly what I have just suggested, while others carried on doing what they had always done and took credit for their figures. Our Force became squeaky clean and ethical, but the figures looked terrible, and we were slated by the Home Office and the Inspectorate who assessed our performance. We were seen as a failing Force and that is the legacy that the Chief handed on to his successor.

For me the Chief had not really thought everything through. He conducted himself like a 'Champagne Socialist', that is, he wanted to be a reformer and a man of the people, but he didn't want to mix with them he just wanted the trappings of the rich and the elite. This was at the time when Tony Blair was just feeling his feet in power and the Chief wanted to be one of his radical disciples. However, in reality he left an unholy mess. If he had written his memoirs, he may have persuaded me that he knew what he was doing but all I inherited from him was a suspicion of all Chief Officers that coloured the rest of my career and perhaps prevented me reaching the very highest ranks of the Police Service.

I will return to crime figures and statistics at a later stage and a lot of things start to link up, so keep your wits about you.

CHAPTER ELEVEN

MARRIAGE

That Assessment Centre was for me a watershed in more ways than one. I had enjoyed the majority of my career up until that point and, perhaps, the enjoyment came from working with people I liked. In reality everything had been off the cuff, light-hearted, steady progress and teamwork. From this point on innocence was over. I moved forward but was increasingly aware that there were potential enemies everywhere.

My father, a police officer before me, had always said (of senior officers).

"They'll put a knife in your back as soon as look at you."

Perhaps I had been lucky or too thick to know what was going on. George Henry (a superintendent who I met earlier in my career) faced me when he tried to destroy my career and it was obvious that the second Chief did not like me. The enemies had been transparent but now they became opaque, and you never knew who your real friends were. In the years that came after this point there may have been Chief Officers who I could have trusted and really got on with, but I just could not identify them, and it became just me and THEM!

Also, not long before the Assessment Centre I had got married. That was the end of living alone with a spaniel for company. Everything was changing all at once or so it seemed. The wedding took place in a lovely old church in November. It was freezing cold and there was snow lying between the gravestones. The temperature was, if anything, lower in the church than it was outside. The vestry roof had been removed for restoration and had been covered with a large plastic sheet. We paid for extra heating, but you could see everyone's' breath condensing into clouds of vapour as they breathed out.

My officers, all in full uniform, lined the driveway to the church entrance and created an extended archway by forming two lines and held their truncheons over my wife and I as we walked out of the church building. There was even a police motor cycle escort for our wedding car. That nice gesture could have turned out be embarrassing. The veteran car which we had hired to convey us to the reception tried to self-destruct and the exhaust fell off while we were surrounded by police officers.

The reception was held in the bar of the station I worked at. It went well, with dozens in attendance including my first Chief Constable and the family who employed my wife as a nanny. To that point all had gone smoothly but the honeymoon was a disaster. We flew from Luton to Funchal in Madeira and had arranged to stop overnight at Luton before our early morning flight. The reception of the hotel looked very impressive in the brochure, and it was supposed to have free car parking where guests could leave their vehicles while they were out of the country. The reality was that the hotel housed homeless people for the local council and every window had bars on them. The car parking consisted of a voucher to use at a car park somewhere else. We were almost late, trying to find the car park in the dark while trying to see through a frozen windscreen.

Things got worse when we realized that my wife's ticket had my surname on it but her passport bore her maiden name. We were still trying to change the name on the ticket long after everyone else had boarded. Then we were told that the flight was delayed and, ticket sorted, we were allowed to walk to the parked plane. It was totally dark at this time in the morning and absolutely freezing, quite literally so, as ice on the wings was the reason the flight had been delayed. We mounted the stairs to the closed door of the aeroplane and. surreally, knocked to be allowed in. As we waited to be admitted we were sprayed with something that came from a passing truck and that, I assumed, was glycol anti-freeze.

Finally, we were allowed to board the plane in time to be informed that everyone could go back to the waiting room in the airport and await further instructions. As we sat, sipping coffee and thawing out, all I could smell was the glycol anti-freeze that we had been doused in.

We eventually took off some four hours later and the flight itself went alright until we landed at Funchal. I am not a good flyer and already knew that the runway in Funchal was the shortest in the EU. As we touched down my wife said, "I've never seen them stop like this before." I looked out of the window next to her and saw that the cowling of the jet engine had come loose and was scraping along the runway. As the cowling broke off there was a dramatic bump and everyone bounced forward in their seats before the plane came to a rather wobbly halt. We were told to remain seated and we waited and waited. We were eventually told to disembark and walk to the airport.

As we stepped onto the runway we were photographed. I noticed that the front of the plane was off the tarmacked strip and the wheel was embedded in loose earth. Another twenty or thirty meters and we would have gone over the end of a cliff and crashed onto Funchal. No one ever apologized or explained exactly what had happened. Nowadays I am sure compensation would have been offered, then I was just glad to be alive.

The hotel was beautiful, all glass and marble with a pianist playing in the Lounge Bar. Outside there was a heated pool from which you could look down on the harbour of Funchal. After the first night I felt terrible. I had a chest infection and my wife, also feeling ill, had a kidney infection. We survived on room service and antibiotics. On CNN TV Channel the Hubble satellite was being retiled. I watched the proceedings for so long I am sure that I could have tiled a satellite if required to do so. After three days my wife went for a swim in the steaming pool. I watched with my coat fastened up to my neck.

An old man walked up to me,

"It's beautiful here, isn't it?" I asked.

"Yes. I've been coming here for forty years, give or take a few." He replied.

"Will you back next year?"

"No. Not next year."

"Are you trying somewhere else?"

"No." He answered and then, "I'll be dead by next year. I've got cancer."

He wandered off leaving me to think of him, the plane landing and my chest infection. The thread that holds us to life felt very thin indeed at that moment.

These pages are supposed to be the memoirs of a senior police officer talking about his career, but I am sure I will have digressed a few times. So having set the scene I will tell you about the romantic, no expense spared, evening I had planned for the last night of our honeymoon. The restaurant was set in a banana plantation and was based in an old, impressive looking building. My wife who could have had steak, prawns, lobster, almost anything, decided she wanted a beefburger! We had both been so ill that we had hardly eaten, and I knew where she was coming from. A beefburger it would be. Two waiters brought it along with 'Hand Crafted Chips' and Mediterranean Paradise Salad. The burger looked wonderful, but it turned out to be raw, indeed the centre was frozen. The next one, that arrived after I complained about the first one, was also raw and my wife declined a third one. They offered a free dessert as an apology, and she accepted that.

A Peach Melba arrived looking wonderful, but my wife could not even cut the peach half with a steak knife! Everything was frozen to the plate. Eventually, very apologetic, the waiters told us that their microwave was broken. No one had checked the food prior to serving it so we called it a day and went back to our hotel where we had peanuts and a few beers. We flew home the next morning.

When I got back to work my first visitor was a total surprise. I had not seen him for some time, and he chatted pleasantly as we sat in my office, but it was obvious that something was the matter. He eventually produced a large black bin liner.

"Some of my friends acquired these at your reception." He stated. "I am so very sorry, and I just knew I should bring them back."

In the bin liner were police helmets, caps, truncheons and even a pair of handcuffs. If the 'friends' had been caught leaving the station with this lot, there would have been nothing I could have done for them. I suspected that the thieves had been women as the lady's toilet was reached through the constables' locker room. However, the way that the items had been concealed must have been impressive, though alcohol will have no doubt helped with a liberal dose of 'Dutch Courage.'

I put the items back, a few at a time, and I am sure the officers who had missed them would have been mightily relieved. The incident smacked of 'Hooray Henrys' and many of those could be found among the friends of my wife's employers. Drink, drugs and rock and roll played a part in the daily life of that group. The mother of the children who my wife worked for was a disaster waiting to happen. On occasions she would take one or two of the children out with her only to return so drunk that she could not remember who she had left the children with.

The mother was clearly unhappy and totally dysfunctional. On one occasion when she was out in her sports car she rang my wife, obviously having been drinking, and she did not know where she was or how to get home. My wife's wages were regularly forgotten, she had to ask for them and then sometimes wait a considerable time before being paid. While my wife waited for her pay, the mother would return home having spent hundreds of pounds on designer clothes.

The husband eventually left, and a boyfriend was moved in. For a time, the situation became even more dangerous for the children. This man was beyond dodgy, he was often described as a drugs dealer, and he certainly was in touch with people who were. He made phone calls stood in the middle of a ploughed field and then he would drive off to collect something. He was regularly high as a kite and his behaviour could be extremely strange.

One day two young girls rode to the house on their ponies to visit one of the children. The boyfriend answered the door and invited the girls in and told them to bring their ponies. The girls resisted the invitation, worrying that the animals might 'poo', but he insisted, and they led the ponies through the kitchen and into a dining room with a sprung wooden floor and left the girls there while he went for the mother. The damage that the iron horseshoes must have done to the floor does not bear thinking about, but I guess in his state of mind that would not even register.

The husband had been the stabilizing influence on the household and when he left the madness went out of his life. Strangely, when the boyfriend eventually cleared off, the mother also started to turn her life round. The whole set up had been Bohemian at best, a nightmare at worst and but for money and my wife the children could have been taken into care. In reality all the children survived and turned out to be good people and well adjusted.

After our marriage my wife could not 'live in' six days a week. She continued to work there, twelve or more hours a day, for a pittance of a wage and she left when her salary was overlooked, and the boyfriend was leaving bottles of urine in the kitchen. Free of the ties to that family we could now start looking for a new home of our own and that was an adventure in itself.

CHAPTER TWELVE

VILLAGE LIFE

We ended up buying a cottage in a working agricultural village. Three large farms dominated the main road that separated the two halves of the settlement. Our home was created when two small estate houses had been knocked into one.

The first time we saw it, the sun was shining and the garden was a picture. We sat among the plants with the people who were selling the cottage. Red wine flowed, music played and we almost had no time to look at the house in the daylight. I think we had already decided to buy it, even before going through the door. They say you should never buy property on cosmetic things, we did and it was the beginning of a love hate relationship with the building that really became a home.

When we got the keys for the house and started to move in we found the whole building to be dirty and run down. Doors were loose on their hinges and your feet stuck to the carpet. The boiler must have come from the Ark and the water ran through the walls without the help of pipes. One day as I sat having my breakfast in the kitchen a jet of water suddenly shot out horizontally from the wall straight into my bowl of cornflakes.

We never did find out where that water came from but one day as I lay in bed the ceiling collapsed on me. Looking up there were gaps in the felting and missing tiles on the roof. I went into the loft and what a mess, all the things that the previous owners had not wanted had been shoved in there. The gaps in the felt had been covered by pieces of cardboard but the whole lot was rotten and the gap between felt and tiles was full of old starling nests.

The wallpaper started to show damp patches which had been artfully concealed by the furniture and pictures of our vendors. The house was a sieve, water came from the roof, up from the ground and through the walls. We reroofed the house, dry lined the walls, decorated every room, replaced every carpet and most of the window frames.

We lived in the pub while the house was made habitable. There we met some great people and some of the strangest characters I had ever met. Our neighbour was called Fenella, a large breasted, fleshy woman with peroxide blond hair.

A man in the pub told me that Fenella had been a 'good time girl' or, more realistically, she had been 'on the game.' My wife and I referred to her as Mrs. Batter, her father, therefore, became Grandad Batter and her daughters were the 'little batters'. Grandad Batter was a small man with a cheeky smile and a twinkle in his eye. He always wore a suit and would display a pocket watch chain. One day when we met him in the pub, he was in the company of a much younger man who without introduction asked, "Do you want a bod box?"

My wife had no idea what a 'bod box' was and she said so.

"It's fer bods, boxes fer bods."

"Where would I put one?" Asked my wife.

"Up a tree like or on a wall."

Only then did it become clear that he was talking about a nesting box for birds. He made them in his spare time as a way of supplementing his beer money. For us the man was always called 'Bod Box'. You always found Grandad Batter and Bod Box in the pub at the same time, they were almost inseparable.

Bod Box worked for the Council Refuse Department, and he could get anything. His house was literally covered in old metal advertising signs. There was one for Colman's' Mustard, a Five Boys Chocolate one, a Camp Coffee sign and at least a dozen of others. His garden was full of old machines and engines. My wife asked where she would find an old Singer Sowing Machine and within two weeks, he turned up with one, a little tired and grubby and it had come from the tip…. but it worked just fine.

Although my wife and I regarded Bod Box as a friendly, amiable eccentric, there were some in the village who regarded his house and garden as an eye sore. One man, Nigel, took a particular dislike to Bod Box as he believed property prices locally were lowered by the state of his house and garden. I must say my sympathy was with Bod Box, Nigel had a plummy voice and was one of those people that, whatever you had done or seen, he had done it or seen it bigger, longer and stronger.

One day Bod Box told me that he had acquired the cockpit and nose cone of an ancient aeroplane. He also had a windsock which came from the same source. I teased Bod Box that if he took down the hedge at the back of his garden, he could use the field behind it as a runway. I did not realise that that lighthearted comment could have such a dramatic outcome.

Bod Box did take down the hedge. He raised the cockpit and nose cone up on old wheelbarrows and he stood two aluminium doors on bricks at each side of the plane parts. He then put up the windsock where the hedge had been. From the other end of the field this strange erection looked to all intents and purposes like an aeroplane. Also, at that end of the field was Nigel's' house!

Nigel came to see me and already knew that I was a policeman. He was full of righteous indignation.

"He's got a plane in his garden. He's dangerous. He'll blow us all up. Can't you do something about him?"

For some reason I do not know why I said what I did. I had no prearranged plan with Bod Box and I knew that Nigel was the sort to make an official complaint if he did not get his own way. I told Nigel that Bod Box was doing everything properly and had applied for a Civil Aviation Licence to fly small planes in and out of the field. I stressed that there was nothing I could do.

"But he can't do that." Pleaded Nigel. He will fly right over my house."

"I don't think it will be a problem." I said warming to the task. "It will only be in the evening and Bod Box has hired a proper pilot."

This exchange triggered more "but, buts" from Nigel who became apoplectic with rage. I should have stopped it there, but he stormed off before I could calm him down. A few days later I had a visit from the Local Authority Planning Department. Nigel had complained and the time had come to explain. Fortunately, the matter did not make it to the Chief Constable, but Nigel never spoke to me again.

All sorts of people came to our house about policing matters even though I did not work in that area. Many of the visitors wanted me to authorize or turn a blind eye to their 'Lamping,' which was a form of poaching. I would certainly not have gone out in the dark near any of that lot with shotguns, but I certainly was not willing to give free range to the hunters. In the end the requests dried up and the local police kept the infringements in check.

Shortly after the Bod Box escapade I was called to see the Chief. I never liked seeing him, as I have already explained, and this time I thought I could be in trouble. When I arrived outside his office there were three other Chief Inspectors waiting to see him. As usual we were kept there for at least half an hour and then all called in at once. I could not now see us all as being in trouble and indeed it was just the opposite. We were all promoted to superintendent forthwith. Usually, we would have been told what jobs we were to be given but this time there was a different twist. We were told that all the Forces' superintending ranks were interchangeable so that one day you could be at a subdivision, the next in CID. That had really always been the case but now we had to wait to see who started off where. At that time, I was in effect a sector commander who was also a superintendent.

A few days later the Assistant Chief Constable (Operations) came to see me. His nickname was 'Crazy Horse', and I was always nervous in his present. He was an amiable enough man, but he had a propensity to fly off into rages of hurricane strength. Fortunately, on this occasion he was in a good mood.

"We want you to be the new Director of Intelligence." He stated and then sat waiting for me to say something.

I didn't know what to say because I didn't know what a Director of Intelligence was. I knew our Force had never had one previously so what was this all about. After what seemed like an eternity Crazy Horse said,

"The Chief wants you to ensure that all our operations are led by intelligence. The idea is that we do not waste time and we do what is needed. We no longer will work on supposition but on real information so that we are guaranteed results on every occasion."

He talked at me for about an hour without saying anything that would have given me a clear idea of exactly what I would be doing. Then, at last, he said the crime intelligence was to be taken away from the CID and management of it would be given to me. There was at least a structure to the way in which intelligence was handled in relation to crime but now intelligence was to belong to everyone and apply to all types of police work.

I suggested that my background did not really give me the best grounding in handling intelligence. His response was promising.

"You are the only one from this round of promotions who has operational credibility. Its' imperative that those doing the job believe in what they are being given. People will be held to account if they do not act on the intelligence you give them and if the CID drag their feet you can report to me."

This was all ego boosting stuff but underlying it all was the Chiefs' desire to emasculate and control the CID. I agreed with the principle, if, for example, bad drivers were causing distress and anxiety in a community then we needed to identify the worst offenders and their vehicles, target them and take them out. Using this approach, we could cut out hours of officers just walking round aimlessly on the chance they might see something.

I must admit that this job was not the one I would have chosen but I could see the challenge and the way forward. However, if I had gathered enough intelligence first, I might have turned the job down and gone back to my sector. I had seriously underestimated the scale of the challenge and the lack of support from Chief Officers.

I had two weeks to wrap up and hand over the job I had been doing. While I was doing that the Force Tailor put crowns on my uniform tunic and I read everything I could on handling intelligence in my spare time. Nothing prepared me for what happened next, and I can still revisit the panic that I experienced on my first day in my new post.

I had not really been told what offices, resources, budget and staff I would have to work with. The Assistant Chief Constable had said that I should turn up for work at the offices which had previously been occupied by the Crime Intelligence Bureau. So, at eight o' clock on a Monday morning I did exactly that and reality hit me like a lump hammer.

The door to what I had assumed would be my new empire was closed and locked. The plaque which had previously identified the offices' function had been unscrewed and removed. I could have gone home and taken the day off for all my presence seemed to mean. As I stood looking at the door a smiling constable in uniform approached me. I knew him from an earlier posting, and he seemed pleased to see me.

"Hello, Sir. I'm your Football Intelligence Officer." He beamed.

"We appear to be locked out." Was my inevitable response.

"Well, I'm the man, Sir, I have a key. I've always had one that they didn't know about."

He unlocked the door and opened it. I would have remained more optimistic if the door could not have been opened! The large room in front of me was completely empty. There were no chairs, no desks, no filing cabinets, no telephones, no computers, the room was completely empty. The walls were stripped of calendars, posters, cork boards and the like. The carpet had been left but it was almost threadbare and the shutters on the windows would neither open nor fully close.

I walked across the wasteland of the office to the far side where there were three more doors. Two of the doors opened to reveal similarly stripped boxes. The third door revealed a veritable palace of comfort. The desk was new, the carpet recent and a coffee machine stood in the corner. This was the Football Intelligence Officers domain, and he informed me that he wouldn't mind if I shared it with him!

A few minutes later the smell of freshly percolated coffee was relaxing me a little. The officer told me that the CID had taken all the office furniture and all the staff apart from him. They hadn't wanted him as he was a uniform officer and responsible for public order and not crime. He was as amazed as I was that they had stripped everything out of the office and we both wondered where the staff, who had previously worked there, had gone.

After a short period of time, I rang the Finance Department to ask them what budget I had been allocated. The situation got worse. They did not know that a new Branch had been created and had no 'budget head' for me and no idea where they could get any extra money from. They said they would look into it!

I then went to the stores to see if they had anything that I could commandeer. I returned with a promised delivery date for some second-hand furniture and equipment, I also managed to divert some new items that the CID had ordered.

A few hours had passed back in the deserted office when I received a visitor from a detective superintendent.

"This won't last." He said. "You've no idea what you're doing or how we did things here. You are stuffed unless you play ball with us."

Now the almost overwhelming feeling of frustration and anger that I had experienced when I first arrived at the offices resurrected itself. I felt like resorting to physical violence but from somewhere came a breath of reason.

"I think we should both go and see the Assistant Chief Constable, don't you?" I said and stood up before walking out of the office towards the Chief Officers 'corridor'. Somewhere along the journey my adversary disappeared but I continued anyway. I knocked on the Assistants office door, without first approaching his secretary, and in consequence ended up sat talking to him within minutes of the CID visit.

He seemed genuinely amazed that all the staff had been withdrawn and we both realised that the Force now had no recognizable intelligence capacity at all. He promised that he would talk to Personnel Branch and see what staff could be made available. He wanted to know how many staff I would need, and I had to tell him that at that time I had no idea because I had not yet got a clear idea of what the new creation would look like. I did say that the first priority was to maintain the old service that had operated out of the offices that I now occupied and to do that I would require the former staff back as a starting point. Further, while I tried to get an angle on all the sources of information that the Force had, we needed state of art computers and I was not the person to acquire those as I could barely switch one on. I definitely needed a right-hand man who knew about computers and had a thorough understanding of the Force Crime Information System.

I think I left the Assistant shell shocked with the scale of what the Force was unleashing, but he did give me the authority to go and find an inspector to work with me. The battle lines had been drawn, I either had to find a way forward or disappear under this mess that the CID had left behind.

I had learned from my time in the Research Services Branch that Chief Officers rarely had original thought. They had all heard of something or seen something that they wanted exploring further or introducing into their area of command. If I was right about that then there had to be something out there that was driving the urge to reform the handling of intelligence. Surely it could not just be the Chiefs' desire to emasculate the CID.

It did not take long to discover that the HMI's (Inspectorate) office had published a paper recommending exactly the sort of thing I had been asked to do. I had a blueprint. Also, my currently non extant unit had been placed under the overall command of a Chief Superintendent and I now had another ally. I would still argue, to this day, that the change in structure of this size should have been Project Managed by a designated team and not handled by a total amateur in the field. However, looking back at it I enjoyed the process from this point.

I knew someone who had a good knowledge of the working of the Forces' computer systems. He had been a detective but at the time he was a uniform sergeant. I was certain that he could provide the hands-on expertise. I had been told that I could have an inspector and was pretty certain that the Chief would not want to promote someone straight into a job of the nature I required. I should have written a job description and completed a skills profile then advertised and conducted a selection process. All that would have taken at least three months and things would have moved a long way by then.

I saw the superintendent in charge of the sergeant I wanted and he arranged for the officer to be temporarily promoted to inspector. A week later I got my new, if temporary, inspector. Three weeks later his promotion was made permanent and I now had two members of staff, some furniture, telephones, a coffee machine and we were up and running.

I could write a book on how to set up a brand-new Branch, but it would be more of a text than a general read. It would certainly bore the pants off a lot of people. In broad terms the task was massive.

Firstly, we searched all the Forces' systems for data and information. We introduced a structure to enable intelligence to drive operations. We did that by creating an intelligence unit at each Division with my unit at Headquarters providing support and guidance. We realized that we needed a computer system that could map and analyse crime and incidents. We recognized that we needed a substantial number of analysts to operate whatever new computer we got.

While we struggled with getting things up and running, we had to work on wildlife intelligence, prison intelligence, liaison with other Forces, intelligence from telephone usage, the tasks seemed to mount by the hour. Someone once said that you have to eat elephants in small pieces and, I guess, that means eating a whole one, at once, would overwhelm you! We tried to create an intelligence system in pieces, we didn't always create them in the right order but eventually things started to take shape.

One of the first tasks was to recruit analysts and as we had never had them before we had to come up with a job description and specification that we could recruit to. Everything needed micromanaging because we were the only people working on it. Our advertisement for Analysts attracted over eight hundred applications for the initial fourteen posts, so just identifying who we were going to interview took several days.

Having sorted out who would attend the interviews we started looking at what training could be given to those who were selected. Further it was necessary that the computers were in place for them to work on when they had been trained.

The new computer system, hardware and software, was going to cost in excess of a million pounds and the Chief Officers left me and my right-hand man to manage the acquisition. Thank goodness for my right-hand man. I liked the demonstration by the chosen supplier, but I had no idea how the system worked, and I kept well away from the keyboards.

Slowly, bit by bit the intelligence function started to take shape. In some ways it became a bit of a secret society. We created an Intelligence Users Group which was a meeting that everyone from Divisional and the Headquarters Units attended. We raised the problems to start with and someone would come up with a 'best fit' solution. Eventually the Divisional units brought their own problems and concerns until, most of the time, the creaking whole started to create a product....that is, it started to direct police operations.

As soon as the packages started to reach operational units the demand started to grow and the anxiety feeling of the early days came back again. The production of intelligence packages was very labour intensive, and we were in danger of being swamped. We created an Operations User Group Meeting so that all the operational units could have their say and we could prioritise what they needed. Both intelligence and operational functions became better aware of each other's capabilities. Sadly, it became obvious that the resources available to the various intelligence units could never drive the Force in the way that had been envisaged. It did start to create quality packages to deal with the more serious crime and public order, but the day-to-day information was a little sporadic to say the least.

My own job grew, even when the structure and staffing started to fall into place. One part of that growth was the requirement to attend meetings at all the prisons in my Force area. Each prison had their own intelligence officers who alerted us to prisoner's release dates, they also recorded which criminals 'associated' with whom. Our Force also assisted with the movement of 'Star Criminals' from prison to prison or prison to court.

I remember one prisoner was to be taken from a maximum-security prison to Crown Court some sixty or seventy miles away. This prisoner was one of the 'elite' of the crime world. He had made a fortune from his life of crime and there was a real fear that there would be an attempt to rescue him when he was moved to court. The intelligence was almost unbelievable.

The suggestion was that a group of criminals would close the motorway between exits. They would then attack the convoy escorting the prisoner before escaping with him on a helicopter.

In reality the scenario changed dramatically as the criminal suffered a serious heart attack in the prison and having made a partial recovery, he was transferred to another prison out of our area. Everyone breathed a sigh of relief.

One strange piece of information came to my attention during the panic just outlined. The police had managed to put a covert camera in the criminals' mansion. The film produced was of quite a good quality. I never saw any footage that showed serious criminals plotting the motorway snatch but what I did see was, if anything, even stranger.

The criminals' house had a full-sized snooker table in the room that was covered by the camera and his son played on it regularly. On one occasion a friend visited for a game, and everyone immediately recognized him as a high-profile professional footballer. I cannot mention his name and there was no suggestion that he was in any way involved with the criminal activities planned there but almost certainly you will have seen him plying his trade. Yet again this showed to me the thin divide in society between the good, bad and dodgy.

One of the establishments located in our Force area had a high security wing. I had visited this when it was being refurbished and I found the facilities similar to a four-star hotel. There were two television rooms, two jogging machines, a full array of training equipment. Individual rooms/cells, a private room to meet visitors in and a small garden to work in. Most surprisingly of all, as far as I was concerned, was a fully equipped kitchen and a collection of cooks' knives that would have graced an Egon Ronay establishment. I suppose that the only reminder to the inmates that they were prisoners was the fact that the garden and outside area was enclosed in a cage to prevent a helicopter being used to affect an escape.

While I was in charge of the Force Intelligence Bureau the Government decided to repatriate IRA prisoners to Ireland. Several of those held in the secure wing fell into that category. The movement of these prisoners was supposed to be top secret.

At an intelligence meeting I was informed that the IRA men were to be flown out of a local airport in a chartered jet. To keep the chances of that information leaking to a minimum I decided to take personal command of the Firearms Operation which facilitated the transfer to the plane.

When I arrived at the airport there were hardly any passengers in the lounge and there were few flights scheduled to come in or depart within the relevant time. Half an hour before the convoy arrived a number of people started to gather around the entrance to the airport. A quick check to identify them revealed that they were all accredited journalists and cameramen. It was obvious that the transfer had been known.

It was too late to divert the convoy as it was only a few miles from the airport. This had been a massive breach of security. The cameramen were armed with their massive telephoto lenses, but I hoped beyond hope that no one had anything more dangerous.

We arranged for the convoy to enter the airport by a gate not open to the public and the vehicles drove onto the edge of the runway. As this happened the media jostled to gain a better advantage point. I positioned myself near the airplane that was to take them to Ireland and from there I saw four very ordinary looking men assisted from the vans.

Each of the prisoners was handcuffed to a warder and one pair at a time mounted the stairs set against the side of the plane. As the last prisoner reached the top of the stairs he turned, pulled his jacket open and waved at the media. I could clearly see the logo on the sweatshirt he was wearing, it said, "Tiz he himself. Back again."

Not only had the media been tipped off but clearly the prisoners knew as well. In all likelihood the IRA establishment would have known that this process was a step in bringing their colleagues nearer home. There was probably little chance of an escape attempt, as this would have endangered the peace programme, but it was a nerve-wracking experience for those involved on the day.

A strange footnote to the transfer was that a handgun was found in a litter bin in the airport lounge. It was wrapped in silver paper, but it was loaded, and tests showed it was a viable weapon. Once again it must be said that the weapon was unlikely to have been intended for use in an escape attempt. It was much more likely that a passenger had been carrying the gun for other purposes and had suddenly seen all the armed officers and jettisoned it in panic. For me it did raise a concern that someone thought they could bring a gun into or out of our local airport, but I know things have changed drastically since then.

Everything that we did in the intelligence unit seemed like breaking new ground and learning from the beginning. People brought problems to us that we initially had no answers to. We now had four sergeants with the grand title of Field Intelligence Officers. They did some good work, but they were all 'hands on' police officers and they were learning the job as they went along, just like my right-hand man and I did.

One area that I really struggled with were the technical issues that constantly arose with our Crime Information System (CIS). I have already said that my IT skills were, to say the least, limited. However, it must be said that the CIS was not fit for purpose. It was a system that had existed for more than a decade and although it had been upgraded it was more of a statistic and recording tool than a proactive intelligence one. I must also say that with the exception of a very few computer aficionados no one really knew how it worked.

What we needed was a computer that we could search to find patterns, to make links between people and most of all to get that information quickly. For those purposes it was useless. One man in the IT Department could search the system by using a tool that I think was called 'Easy Spec Dargle.' The name must have been a misnomer. The search would take all night to find one piece of information and if we only had one person who could do it then easy it was not!

Our first task had been to find a way of mapping crime, leaving the CIS problems to those in the IT Department and the Crime Investigation Department who 'owned' the CIS. Nothing was going to be easy, but we did find a company who could download information from the CIS and transfer it onto a programme that would give us a usable product. Unfortunately, the patterns were emerging late, a criminal could have moved on before we identified it, but it was a good start.

A further problem was the Data Protection Legislation. As a member of the public, I have never liked public bodies and companies holding swathes of personal information. Nowadays computers know everything about us down to the brand of toothpaste we are most likely to use. Well, the Data Protection Legislation sought to place a check on what information public bodies, such as the Police, were legally allowed to hold.

Everyone would, I think, recognize that the Police will hold information about convictions, cautions and the like. However, we also hold information that is a little more vague. If a police officer sees Billy, the Burglar, having a drink with Fred the Fence then that may well get recorded. We will also record what vehicle he drives and where it was seen, that and a whole host of other personal information.

The legislation does not stop the Police holding that sort of information, but it does set certain criteria that must be met. So, the information has to be timely (recent), relevant, proportionate and other such terms. If Billy is seen having a drink with an unknown female, then it may be sound to record it but certainly it should not be held on record a year later. Thus, if a piece of information is out of date or no longer relevant then it should be deleted.

The legislation terrified the police staff who were responsible for inputting and deleting the information. They were given a brief training input and sent back to work believing that they must delete everything that is more than a few weeks out of date. Our own experts went out and performed audits of the data we were holding, and this increased the paranoia that the staff were suffering from. Officers on the street were pouring information into the system and those operating the computers were deleting it as quickly as it was put on.

It was not long before the sergeants from the Divisional Intelligence Bureaux brought their concerns to the Force Intelligence User Group Meetings. There was a real sense of desperation and I drafted a report to the Assistant Chief Constable who was responsible for my area. As usual reports in the Police go on a long and tortuous voyage before coming back to the originator. In this case the report had gone to the Head of CID, the Force Solicitor, the Head of the IT Department and then had been an item at the Chief Officers Meeting.

The result of that journey was, basically, there could be no change. Everything turned on the views of the Force Solicitor who emphasized that the Force was doing everything required by the legislation. When I took this message back to the sergeants, I was faced with a near mutiny situation. I had to find a way of making the system work or we may just as well throw the intelligence from street officers into a large waste bin.

I had several meetings with the Assistant Chief Constable. I visited a number of other Forces to see what they were doing, and I spent time with the Force Solicitor. It was all like banging my head on the wall again. The view of other Forces was that they left it to the operatives, and they took the risk if they did not delete what they should do. I could find no blueprint that would help us find a solution. I even tried an unusual approach. J Edgar Hoover was the Director of the FBI in the US. He was an immensely powerful individual who allegedly taped Presidents so that he had leverage with them. I had read a book about Hoover and took it with me to a meeting with the Assistant Chief Constable and I left it with him. I suppose I was hoping he would think I was keeping tracks on him, but it didn't help us find a solution.

We were sleeping walking towards a disaster, using an outdated computer, maintaining it intensively and then rendering it useless by deleting its content. If I had had nothing else to do, I suppose I could have been even more of a nuisance, but the policing world was moving very quickly, and saturated workloads tend to dull the effectiveness of even the best units.

Among the many extra duties that I acquired at this time was a requirement to review investigations into major crime. I am not certain how I qualified to perform that function as I had never attended any CID training. I did, however, enjoy getting stuck into the detail of investigations and particularly liked watching senior detectives squirm when a novice found them to have missed something!

To be honest I was amazed at the length to which investigators went and the professionalism with which they applied themselves. It also became clear the senior investigating officers took failures as a personal affront and would return to undetected cases time and time again. I remember one case where a young boy had been murdered and his body disposed of in a local canal. That case haunted the memories of all who had been involved in the initial investigation and years later with the help of DNA technology the offender was traced.

One of the reviews I conducted was a strange one. A company operated a hot air balloon and 'flew' people on short trips. I had always fancied floating through the air with a panoramic view of the scenery below. It struck me that it would be a peaceful, relaxing and exhilarating way to travel. The demand for such flights was great and the trips were often bought as gifts for those celebrating birthdays, anniversaries, retirements and the like.

The company in the case I was tasked to review operated a flight over the large estuary which separated the two parts of our Force area. The balloon was planned to take off from the grounds of a well-known hotel and the 'fliers' gathered early for refreshment prior to departure. The pilot of the balloon conducted the safety checks, including researching the weather conditions and take off went well. Things started to go wrong almost immediately as the balloon did not reach the required height and soon a decision was made to return to base at the hotel. Getting lower and lower the balloon landed in what must have seemed a really precarious location as it was immediately next to a railway line. After a short delay the pilot took off again but once more could not gain sufficient altitude and the balloon drifted over the fields next to a built-up area.

By now the passengers must have realized that things were not going particularly well and that balloons were not as controllable as they might have hoped. I can only imagine the terror of those on board as the balloon drifted onto the electric cables that carried the local power supply. A death, burns and serious injuries were the result. The question for the police was whether or not the company had behaved negligently in organizing the flight. Particularly, there was the question of whether or not a local radio weather forecast was sufficient for these purposes.

The senior investigator had contacted a host of experts in aviation and my review took me to the headquarters of the Civil Aviation Authority. That place was a museum of the horrors of flying. There were examples of engineering problems that had downed commercial jets through to the neglect of amateur fliers who did not take things seriously enough. However, for me the most chilling thing/exhibit was a reconstruction of a famous plane.

As I entered a large hangar, stood against the far wall was what looked like a battered Jumbo jet. In reality this was the reconstruction of the Pan Am 103 flight that had crashed into Lockerbie in 1988. As I got nearer to it the size of the thing was a little overwhelming and then I realized that it was one dimensional, like a jigsaw put together in flat pieces. To think that an explosion at thirty thousand feet had caused the plane to crash into the ground at approaching five hundred miles an hour and left enough to create that illusion.

All the passengers on Pan Am 103 died, as did eleven residents of Lockerbie. It is one of those events, like the death of John Kennedy and the Hillsborough Disaster, that leave you remembering where you were when it happened. I had also heard at the time of a police officer who was one of the first at the scene. He checked the wreckage for any survivors and wandered over a wide area before collapsing an hour or so after his arrival. It was found that the plane had been carrying a consignment of surgical needles and the officer had walked through them. They had penetrated his wellingtons and embedded themselves deeply in his feet but he never realized that it had happened until he woke up in hospital. Shock can have an incredible impact on peoples' lives even when it leaves no visible signs.

I am getting side tracked. The investigation into the balloon disaster had been conducted properly but you can imagine how long it takes to check on the actions of a team and then writing a report which could be as long as the original paperwork. I must have done the review work well enough because I believe it was this that led to a strange offer.

I had been a superintendent for approaching two years and had been Director of Intelligence for all of that time. Then one day I received a phone call asking me to come and see the Deputy Chief Constable immediately. I had no idea what this was going to be about. If anything, I suspected it would be because of the feathers I had ruffled in trying to resolve the problems with the Crime Information System and intelligence retention.

He asked if I wanted a cup of coffee and then he launched immediately into the reason for calling me.

"I want you to apply for the vacancy of Detective Chief Superintendent."

Then he sat there waiting for a reply. I am sure he must have expected that I would snap his hand off to get that job. This was one of the senior posts in the Force; it would involve further promotion and it would provide a really serious challenge as the Chief was still engaged in 'cleaning up' the CID.

My response was clearly not what he expected and in retrospect I should have welcomed the request with enthusiasm. I had only served in the CID at the most junior level, I had never commanded detectives, nor had I interviewed a murderer or topflight criminal. I had always liked to lead from the front and how could I if I had never even attended a course in the basics. It was a nerve-wracking prospect and one that I did not have the confidence to confront.

He told me that I should think about it and think carefully because my future could depend on it. That was clear enough then! I went home and talked to my wife, and she felt that I should be flattered because some people thought I could do it. I knew the others who would also throw their hats into the contest for the post and, in my opinion, one of them was the obvious candidate. It seemed wrong that he should be denied what was seen as his destiny by the Chiefs' obsession with reforming the CID.

I went to find out when the interviews were to take place and I was informed that a date had not yet been determined but they had to be held within a period of ten days. I went to a travel agent and booked a two-week holiday to Tunisia. There, that was the very mature response that I came up with to a problem that was burning my head.

Looking back, years later, I know I should have gone to the interview. The heir apparent got the job because, as it was explained to me later, in my absence there was no real competition. The Deputy called me in to his office again as soon as I landed back in the Force area. He was frosty and annoyed. He was also very candid. The new Detective Chief Superintendent had been seen as too much one of the boys and a member of the 'old guard'. He had headed up a team at one time that became known as the local 'mafia' not because they were dishonest but because of the 'one for all, all for one spirit'. The crime figures from that unit were excellent but there was a doubt about the ethics of the techniques used in recording the data and this was exactly what the Chief had wanted to eradicate.

If the Chief had not held me in the highest esteem prior to this, then my act of sabotage had undoubtedly gained me another black mark. The CID had caused me no end of problems when I took over the intelligence function from them and they had not helped much since my new unit got up and running. If nothing else, I could have given some of my biggest adversaries a hard time as their 'boss'. I should have gone for it and, however I dress it up, the real reason was a lack in confidence.

It was round about this time that I experienced another aspect of being a senior officer. I had been told, when I first joined, that there would be some who would be jealous of my having gained a place on the Accelerated Promotion Scheme. I had only ever been the subject of that jealousy from a senior officer, George Henry, my boss when I was a newly promoted sergeant. My peers and lower ranks were never anything other than welcoming and friendly. To me, being in the police was like being in a family but I was about to see the darker side.

I was forty years of age by this time, but I still played rugby and managed to defy the years from a fitness point of view. When I could not play away with the local first team, I captained the second team at home. The clubhouse was a warm friendly place and I guess the whole set up made it the perfect way of forgetting police work and unwinding. Unfortunately, policing was about to follow me into this protective domain.

Ewan Sutcliffe was an inspector and I had known him for a number of years. His main claim to fame in the Police was his commitment to bringing discipline charges against as many junior officers as possible. He talked in a staccato manner like a machine gun going off and his favourite phrase, "I'll run him", was somehow iconic (to 'run' someone basically meant to prefer charges against someone).

He was a strange man with an aura of sleaziness about him. As a constable I was called to suspicious 'goings on' at a local licensed premises. When I arrived, there were several cars in the car park, but the lights were off in the pub and the doors were locked. I went to look at the cars and each vehicle had a couple in it. The first car which I checked belonged to Ewan Sutcliffe and when I knocked on a side window, I did not recognize the man in the vehicle. Both occupants were almost naked, and it was obvious what they had been up to. The lady in the car turned out to be Mrs. Sutcliffe, the man with her said that Ewan was in another car nearby with his wife. All the cars were occupied by members of a local wife swapping club. Most people caught in these circumstances by a work colleague would have been embarrassed but Ewan reminded me of it every time we met, and he thought it was hilarious.

There were all sorts of similar stories passing around the Force but one I liked did not have sexual connotations. I had no involvement with what I am about to relate but I was told about it in great detail by a Detective Chief Inspector I worked closely with, and for this purpose we shall call him Gary.

Gary and his wife were middle aged, their children had recently left home and they decided that the time was right for a romantic few days in a remote location. They decided upon the Tatra Mountains between Slovakia and Poland, and it certainly was remote. The hotel was in a pine forest and at the time of the year they expected there to be snow.

The hotel that they arrived at was made of wood and resembled a larger version of those hill farm buildings you see on boxes of Swiss Chocolates. The snow was deep when they arrived and a storm soon provided a lot more, they looked likely to be cut off there. Log fires roared in the lounge and restaurant and as they enjoyed a glass of wine a violinist appeared at their table and showed no sign of leaving any time soon. It was obvious that only a handful of people were stopping at the hotel, and they felt relaxed in the idyllic atmosphere.

Shortly after they had ordered their evening meal the door to the outside world swept open and a flurry of snow blew into the room. Two figures stumbled in after the snow. They looked, to all intents and purposes, like snow sculptures. Shuffling and stamping they began to look more human as the staff rushed to their assistance. The door was closed, and the pair were led towards the fire. Suddenly Gary heard the couple distinctly speaking English but more significantly he thought he recognized at least one of the voices. Then he heard, "Hey, Mary. Look who's here. It's Gary Lund. Bugger me!"

Gary realized immediately that it was Ewan Sutcliffe, the moment of tranquillity was ruined for good. The couple plonked themselves down at their table and they remained there for the whole evening. Gary felt like the scene from Casablanca when Rick questions the arrival of his ex-lover in his bar, "of all the bars in all the world". It was difficult for Gary to conceal his animosity towards Ewan and for the rest of their stay he and his wife hid from the late arrivals.

Ewan had been caravanning in Poland and had driven off the road quite near the Hotel. If they had had the mishap anywhere else in that area, they could well have frozen to death. Gary probably wished they had! Several hundred miles from home and he ends up sitting next to one of the people he liked least in the whole world.

Ewan was a rugby referee. He was not particularly good at it, but in amateur rugby circles you had to take whoever was allocated the matches' officiating role. As a captain I had to greet the referee and ensure he got his match expenses, received a drink and was fed before he left. It was Ewans' refereeing of a game at my club that removed the peace and warmth of the clubhouse retreat. I was about to experience the sort of feeling that Gary had gone through but with slightly more sinister overtones.

I was going out after the game on that particular night so I hoped Ewan would not overstay his welcome. Sadly, he seemed well set and was taking advantage of the cheap beer available at the club. I had bought him a drink, turned down his offer to reciprocate and I was only drinking shandy as I had to drive home.

Not long before I left, I stumbled into Ewan as I left the toilets which he was entering. He made some sort of comment about one of us not being able to take their beer, but I knew that it was certainly not me. I drove out of the car park and onto the dimly lit country road that led to the nearby village. I had only travelled a couple of miles when a blue light suddenly lit the night behind me. I slowed and the Police car overtook me, then to my surprise it slowed in front of me, so I had to do so eventually coming to a halt behind the now stationary vehicle in front.

The officer told me that he had reason to believe that I had alcohol in my body and he required a sample of breath for a breathalyser to determine if I was over the prescribed limit. I knew I would not be. An orange juice, and two glasses of weak shandy over an hour and half would not put me over the limit. I asked what had attracted the officers' attention and he said it was my manner of driving. I failed to see what that involved as I had left a car park, turned right and then driven in a perfectly straight line to the point where I was stopped.

The breathalyser test was negative, as I'd suspected. The officer was most apologetic, but he did say that the alcohol had probably not worked through my system yet. That is nonsense as breath alcohol is present and measurable straight away and only blood alcohol levels continue to rise before falling when you stop drinking.

I drove on feeling a little annoyed and wondering what the real reason had been for stopping me. I had hardly done another two miles when I was stopped by a second police car with the same result. This time I did point out that I had just been breathalysed and I wondered if this did not have a little overkill about it. Once again, the test was negative. I again asked why I had been stopped and this time the officer blatantly informed me that a friend had reported seeing me drink excessively in the rugby club. As soon as this was said I knew who it was. Ewan was obsessed with 'running' people and I would be fair game in spite of our having been socializing together. At a later time, when I pressed him, he admitted that he had called the incident in to the police. He thought it was an enormous joke, but you can be assured I was not laughing at the time or afterwards.

The whole incident reminded me of the strange unreality of police work. I know and many members of the public know that the police regularly fail to turn up to reports of disorder and crime. Yet here two officers were available to breathalyse a colleague twice in ten minutes. Also, in a strange way the incident had stained the peace of my one bolt hole, it seemed like I was a fair target as a superintendent and the world did not quite seem the same anymore.

The days of innocence were well and truly over. I had always regarded myself as one of the 'worker bees' and not part of management. That in reality had ceased to be the truth a long time ago. I was no longer 'one of the boys'; no one told me who was doing what to whom anymore and the invitations to booze ups and parties had started to dry up. What was true was that I did not feel comfortable in the management circles with their airs of self-importance and superiority. I was becoming a little isolated and a less effective police officer as a result.

My least favourite Chief Constable, whom I had started referring to as 'the Limp Chief', was still in charge of the Force at this time. I had hardly had a conversation with him since I took over Intelligence and the rift between us was clearly still there. However, his favourite (a blond male who set fire to his fringe in my earlier book) was wanted at Headquarters to work on Corporate Development. He had already had a posting to the FBI Training Centre at Quantico and an attachment to Chris Patton at the time of Britain's' returning Hong Kong to China, it was nepotism gone mad but this time his upward mobility had a spin off for me.

I had always wanted to be a Divisional Commander and the posting of the blond one to Corporate Services left a vacancy at one of the Forces' four Divisions. I threw my name into the hat and was immediately given the job, but nothing went smoothly for me while the 'Limp Chief' was around.

Previously the Chief had stated that all his superintendents were interchangeable and, therefore, becoming a Divisional Commander would have been a sideways move. But now it became a promotion and there would have to be a competitive interview. I was given the job on a 'temporary' basis, so in many ways this was a poison chalice because if I did anything wrong, they could get rid of me straight away but if I was good at it I still had to get through the selection process. How many times would the playing field change under one Chief.

So, I said "goodbye" to my team in Intelligence and was immediately replaced by a superintendent who was posted there permanently. If things did not work out at the Division, then I would have a new job whatever happened.

CHAPTER THIRTEEN

DIVISIONAL COMMAND

I was to become responsible for the policing needs of a population of 168,000 people. The Police Division covered the same area as the local Council (Unitary Authority). I had some two hundred and fifty police officers and fifty civilian support staff under my command and, though that might sound a lot, we were fairly thinly spread.

I was informed on my arrival that the Division covered 85,000 hectares. Let me tell you now that I had no idea what that area looked like, and I still cannot get my head round the dimensions of a hectare. I have a vague grasp of an acre (somewhere you could keep a pony, or which is just about big enough to plough!) but I do know that an area forty miles by twenty miles at its widest points was pretty big.

The area covered was largely rural with a number of small to medium sized market towns and one large urban conurbation. It was a very long way from the sleepy backwater that it seemed from afar. The urban area had been based round the steel industry and that still persisted.

The Headquarters was based in the large urban centre. There was a substantial police station built around an adequate car park and garaging area. Also, across the road, there was one of those small tower blocks built of concrete and glass in the late 1960's. My office was on the third and top floor of the tower block, it must have been one of the best offices in the whole Force. You could have held a dance in the room it was so large, and three walls were wood panelled. The fourth wall was completely glass with a view over the police station below. There were two built in wardrobes and another cupboard concealed a large bar. It seemed like an executive penthouse suite and for the first time I had my own secretary, someone I came to rely on totally in the coming months.

The office may well have been a perk, but the job was huge. I will go into the number of meetings I had to attend a little later and then there were all the day to day personnel issues of such a large workforce to deal with. However, the worst thing was that you retained an operational command responsibility while managing such a large area. There can be few jobs where you can be in a meeting with the Chief Executive of another organization and be called out to deal with, for example, a firearms incident. It was like doing two jobs at once. For seven days every month I was the operational cover for two Divisions twenty-four hours a day while the management role in my own Division was there all the time.

On average, I would be called out for something every other night. Often the calls were to visit the Charge Office at the station to review the continued detention of a prisoner, but in my case the attendance involved a seventy-mile round trip from my home to the station. I once got called out three times in one night, one of them to a serious public order incident. The third time I just stopped in my office and one day ran into another without the chance of sleep for forty-eight hours. On several occasions I slept on the floor of my office, and I started keeping a sleeping bag there. The job certainly required total commitment.

I seemed to be at work much more than I was at home but in spite of this I heard some of my staff saying that they never saw me. I suppose the meetings were a part of that as many of them took place at Force Headquarters over forty miles away and the fact that my office was not in the main police station also compounded the feeling. But if the staff felt I was not there much, then collectively. they were always there for me. On a regular basis there would be an issue between individuals which started as a minor event and quickly blew into a major one that was time consuming to resolve.

I remember one constable who decided that his sergeant adopted a superior attitude when allocating tasks to him. Then on one occasion he decided he didn't think he should carry out a task, was subsequently ordered to do it and again refused. The constable complained before the sergeant could and the Police Federation (Police 'Union') became involved.

The constable wanted the sergeant disciplining for being rude towards him and the Federation supported his case. I was asked if I would arbitrate between the two officers involved. I researched the incidents that had caused the dispute to erupt and could find nothing wrong with the sergeants' behaviour. The constable had a reputation for being disruptive and the tasks he was asked to perform were perfectly normal duties.

I reminded the Federation representative that both officers were members of the Federation. I also pointed out that the constable had previously served in the army and had been used to a disciplined environment. There were witnesses to what had happened and no one thought the sergeant had behaved in an untoward manner. I asked both parties what they wanted, and the sergeant wanted the constable to do what he was asked while the constable wanted the sergeant moving from the shift he worked on.

I offered the constable the chance to move to a different relief or station, as that would resolve the issue, but he responded by saying that I would be punishing him because his work pattern would change. The situation was becoming a stand-off. I would not be seen to punish the sergeant while I could move the constable but that would only result in a further complaint. As so often, an opportunity arose that provided a way out. The sergeant had been in the CID for years prior to his promotion and he clearly wanted to go back there. A vacancy arose in the CID, and I arranged for the sergeant to fill it. The sergeant was happy, but the constable was still unhappy as he felt the sergeant was being rewarded. It was like dealing with children, and at that time I snapped. I informed him in no uncertain terms that I had made my decision. Nothing further happened. I knew I had a trouble causer in the station, but he clearly could not complain about his supervisors again as he would be establishing a pattern of behaviour.

All of that seems to be very trivial after the many years that have passed since the incident involved. However, at the time it was very time consuming and the whole Division seemed to be watching to see if the constable could win. Before that problem had been resolved another personnel issue arose that definitely was not trivial.

The second personnel issue that I will recount did get out of hand. It began in a strange manner as a 'slow burner' that simmered for a long time before exploding dramatically.

Soon after my arrival as Divisional Commander my office door burst open and a young female in civilian clothes literally bounced into the room. I had no idea who she was, what she was or what she wanted. She walked around the room, as if visiting a museum or art gallery, then stopped in front of my desk.

"Hello. You're the new Commander? I'm R--."

She sounded on edge, so I asked her to sit down. Her response was unusual in the extreme.

"Can I sit on the floor? I've got bum cramp?"

I wanted to ask what that was as the surreal visit started to play out in front of me. However, I quickly realized that bum cramp must be just like any other cramp as my visitor contorted and twisted her body in front of me. These activities involved regular glimpses of upper thigh and a bare mid riff as I quickly became unsettled in my own office.

"Do you know who I am?" She asked.

I replied in the negative as she began to take over the already one-sided conversation.

"I'm the looney from downstairs. I've been working here for a while, but I think I'm OK now. I've got a degree. When can I get promoted now that I'm sorted out?"

Slowly and surely the verbal transaction between us became more normal. It transpired that she had been, in her own estimation, a normal, efficient officer who had passed her promotion examinations. Then she had some sort of breakdown which had resulted in her being away from work and she was now easing herself back into a daily routine. She was employed in one of the Divisions' specialist units and enjoyed being there, but she confided that her husband was keen for her to get promoted as soon as possible.

I would have sooner heard that the husband was supporting her recovery rather than pushing her for promotion, particularly as the breakdown had followed the birth of their first child. I agreed to have a look at her file and that we could then meet again. She then levered herself up off the floor and bounced out of my office as flamboyantly as she had arrived.

I had been intrigued by this visit, but I was very busy, and it was some days before the next instalment played out when a Chief Inspector visited me and filled in some of the gaps.

The mystery woman was married to a detective sergeant at the Division. He was well thought of according to the Chief Inspector and the couple had seemed normal and happy until the wife gave birth to a boy just over a year ago. On returning to work she had only been back a few days before her behaviour had become strange and she was seen standing on the roof of the Headquarters tower block.

The Chief Inspector had been the first to follow her onto the roof where a discussion resulted in the officer telling him that she had thought of throwing herself off. Fortunately, she allowed herself to be talked out of her intention and she was taken to hospital in an ambulance.

During the conversation with her rescuer, it emerged that the majority of those working at the station thought the woman was as "mad as a bag of frogs". This opinion seemed to be based on the roof incident and an event some months earlier. On that occasion she had been attached to a murder investigation team in another Division. After a day at work, she went for a drink with the team and became too inebriated to drive home. She stopped at a friends' house and surprised that friend when in the middle of the night the visitor got in bed with her and her husband. The behaviour on that night was apparently part of an eccentric pattern.

On checking her file, it became obvious that my peculiar visitor was extremely intelligent and had all the qualifications she told me about at our earlier meeting. Once again, she seemed to drift out of my focus until one day, I was having a meeting with an inspector and an issue relating to her husband cropped up. I had never heard a bad word about the husband until that moment.

The inspector had once run a small station in a rural village at the far west end of my Division. He only supervised four constables and, therefore, had a good appreciation of their abilities and characteristics. The husband was stated to be obsessed with money and he took every opportunity to maximize his overtime earnings. While we agreed that that was not an uncommon trait among police officers the inspector thought that the husband took it to the extreme. He almost always arrested someone just before he went off duty; if he worked a rest day or Bank Holiday, he would ensure there was a reason to stay on duty long after he should have gone home.

It was also mentioned, in passing, that the husband was on wife number two and perhaps most significantly the first wife had had some sort of breakdown. She had made a full recovery after divorcing the husband and was then happily married to a member of the legal profession.

Again, a period of time elapsed and I moved house to a village located in my Division then one day, completely out of the blue, I was visited by PC R--- and her son. It was a pleasant enough visit, but it was strange for a constable to arrive uninvited and unannounced at a Divisional Commanders' house, especially when they hardly knew each other. Further, it transpired that the husband was sat outside in their car during the visit. Very strange, and not the last of these visits and at times it felt as if I was being stalked.

On one occasion I was visited by the Chair of the Police Authority who I had known for many years. Suddenly PC R----- was knocking at the door. She said that she was passing and wanted to use the toilet. Stranger and yet stranger.

After I had been Divisional Commander for two or more years the 'slow burner' took a more serious and sinister turn. I had been told that the couple had split up and the husband had moved out. Then I received a phone call from the wife saying that she had been smoked out of her own home. She claimed the husband had put a wet blanket over the chimney and this had filled the house with smoke. She could not live there and did not know where to go. She felt completely isolated as she felt her parents might take the husbands' side with the events coming so soon after her breakdown.

I do not know if the Fire Brigade was called to the house, and she certainly would not make a formal complaint to the Police. She believed that the husband wanted mother and child out of the matrimonial home so that it could be sold, and the proceeds shared.

I believe that she stayed with a friend for a period of time before one night turning up at a four-star hotel located in the divisional area. Her presence at the hotel became known to the husband and he contacted Social Services to say that the child was in danger with her. While spending a peaceful night she was visited by duty social workers who formed the opinion that the child was safe with his mother. Imagine though the embarrassment of officials arriving at the hotel in the middle of the night, demanding your room number and using legal powers to do so. To me this was a sinister situation as the husband must have used his position as a police officer to elicit the action which was taken.

A few weeks later, when PC R-----had returned to live at her parents, arrangements had been made for the father to have access to his son for a day. The wife also had a hospital appointment on the same day, so things appeared to be working well. Somehow things went wrong and there was a disturbance outside the police station. The result was that the wife was either assaulted, pushed or accidentally shoved and there certainly was a noisy interchange.

I was called and I immediately asked a sergeant to escort the husband to the CID office and sit with him till I sorted out what had happened. The wife would not make a statement and the witnesses, some of them police staff, were surprisingly vague. By the time I got back to the police station the husband had been left in the CID office to his own devices. He had made phone calls to the hospital and social services suggesting that the wife should be 'sectioned' (detained under the Mental Health Act). I was furious because I had said that he should not be left alone.

The case was referred to the Discipline and Complaints Department where it was allocated to an old friend and colleague of the husband. He was posted to another Division shortly afterwards where he quickly rose to the rank of Detective Inspector. I was not happy with the way the situation had been handled and rang his new Divisional Commander. The response was also worrying.

"He's, our officer. He's married to a mad woman and he's doing a good job for us. We'll look after him."

So, my station backed the husband after the disturbance, the 'investigation' was a closed shop, and he was untouchable at his new Division. PC R----- survived but she left the Force and so far, as I know then led a normal life. The husband rose to the dizzy heights of Detective Chief Superintendent, and someone once referred about him to me as "--- nice but dim". I prefer to think of him as "dodgy in the extreme" but then history is written by the winners......however they win.

Another personnel issue that came to me much later in my tenure as Divisional Commander. I had acquired a Detective Chief Inspector who came to me with a good reputation for closing cases successfully. By this time, I had converted much of my Headquarters building into multi agency usage. The Drugs Action Team worked from there as did the Community Disorder Team and the Domestic Violence Unit (all of these bodies were mixed police and civilian staff not employed by the police.). To facilitate this, I had closed the Major Incident Suite which had spent much of each year closed up and unused. There remained one room from which a team could manage murder investigations.

The Detective Chief Inspector did not like the reduction of the CID facilities and he sought every opportunity to make his case against my restructuring of the office accommodation. He claimed that staff from other agencies represented a risk of a security breach, but it became tiresome after several months of the same stale, unevidenced issues being raised.

I remember one incident which did not show the DCI in a particularly good light. I was in a meeting with some senior staff from the Council, meanwhile a teenager was visiting the Drug Action Team as part of his rehabilitation from a period of drug abuse. He asked his supervisor if he could use the toilet and he was accompanied there. Inside the toilet at the urinal was the DCI and the teenager stood next to him to relieve himself.

Seconds later the door to my office burst open and the DCI stood before those assembled in my meeting. His face was bright red, and he was clearly agitated as he said, "I've just stood next to a 'scrote' in the loos." There was shocked silence from those in the room.

It was an amazing outburst in a meeting designed to create better working arrangements across agencies and, as I have already said, the 'scrote' was a client of one of the agencies present. Language like that seemed to take us back weeks and required a whole lot of initiatives designed to rebuild confidence.

Within days I was called to Force Headquarters to explain why criminals were walking about unsupervised in my Divisional Headquarters. It had not taken the DCI long to renew his campaign against the new usage of my building and it did not take me long to inform the Chief Officers that they had been misled by a disruptive influence.

Only a matter of weeks after the toilet issue there was a dispute about the sound proofing in the murder investigation room. That was it. I closed the lot and opened an office in the police station across the road. The sniping continued but the CID must have realized that they had lost the battle, or at least as long as I remained in office.

I must also mention that at this juncture the DCI ended up in front of me again. This time it was to answer a complaint from another senior officer who complained that she had been the subject of sexual harassment and discrimination. The officer complaining wanted the matter kept within the Division but she did want an apology. The DCI once again nearly exploded when I called him in to face the allegations. However, he did apologise, after a fashion, and he moved from the Division shortly thereafter. The DCI was another who went on to become Detective Chief Superintendent and then slid into a senior civilian post in Criminal Justice when he retired from the Police. Eventually he went to prison for sexual offences and I hope there was no limitation placed on which toilet he could use there.

The final personnel issue that I will cover here relates to a complaint made by the Finance and Resourcing Manager based at my Division. His story related to the alleged misconduct of my predecessor who it was claimed had 'cooked the books' in relation to his mileage claims and girlfriends' overtime. The

FARM knew the distance between locations like the back of his hand and he had measured the distance from my predecessors' home to the station personally.

It seemed that the alleged offender was entitled to claim between his home address and his Division. At that time, you could claim travelling costs, for a temporary period, when you were first posted until you could move house. My predecessor had no intention of moving house and had extended the 'temporary' period several times by applying to the Police Authority. He was travelling around a hundred miles a day and was 'earning' a substantial amount of money by doing so.

According to the FARM my predecessor had a girlfriend who lived in the Divisional area and regularly stopped at her house when he was on call. His claims, however, still related to the distance from his home to the Divisional Headquarters. He also authorized his girlfriend working overtime when he worked at a weekend so that they would be on duty together.

I was shown copies of the claim forms, but I had no idea when, if ever, he did stop at his girlfriends'. Further, he had authorized the girlfriends' overtime, but he was empowered to authorize any officer's overtime. Short of passing the whole business to Discipline and Complaints there was nothing I could do and really what could the 'Complaints' do regarding proof of his nocturnal stopovers. The FARM may well have been right and for me it remained an open case.

Sadly, the FARM developed some sort of memory and energy loss which caused him to take early retirement and my predecessor was off the hook. How I would wish I had pursued the missing evidence a little harder when hostilities between us were to erupt in the not-too-distant future. The whole lot was given a strange twist when the alleged offender presented a paper to the Police Authority, this resulted in the abolition of travelling expenses on a permanent posting.

All the issues that I have just related may have triggered a feeling among the readers that we are considering trivia in the greater scheme of things. However, they do provide a flavour of the background against which all the more serious and significant events were taking place. Further, all these events were very important to those taking part in them and they would all have regarded them as significant in their lives and careers.

Finally, I would point out that I originally intended to use the title 'The Good, the Bad and the Dodgy' for this book. There are at least three potentially 'dodgy' individuals mentioned in the cases outlined here. For that reason alone, I believe this chapter to have been worthwhile.

CHAPTER FOURTEEN

POLICING TEAMS AND PARTNERSHIPS

It is now necessary to do a little scene setting for what will come in the ensuing pages. I began my career in an era of flared trousers, droopy moustaches, mullet hairstyles and 'Life on Mars'. Here though we have entered the brave new world of Tony Blairs' 'New Labour Utopia' and Policing was taking on a whole new look and image.

I could not stand Tony Blair as a person. He resembled a grinning Cheshire Cat, dripping insincerity and exuding smarminess in bucket loads. He and his wife, with her mouth painted on the side of her face, definitely fell into that 'dodgy' category. The pursuit of wealth and personal power at all costs seemed to take over completely in his later years as Prime Minister and that undermined everything that could have been achieved.

However, though I had no time for him as a human being I definitely liked many of the policies that he and his party espoused. Primarily, I loved the Crime and Disorder Act which launched officially the way of working that I had championed for years.

The essence was partnership working. All agencies of local government were tasked with contributing to solving crime and disorder problems as part of their daily work. Resources rained down on the partnerships as if Gordon Brown had a bottomless pit of money. I loved it, at least I did in the beginning before it went too far, and the wheels started to come off the wagon. In reality there was no pit and as the funding dried up the structures began to creak and crumble and now after years of Tory austerity there is very little of it all left.

The golden years of partnership lasted for about ten years and it did show what could be achieved. This period coincided with my becoming Divisional Commander and although I was familiar with working in an environment similar to that now created by legislation, we all had to learn a new management language and familiarize ourselves with the structures and working of local government. Many of us, including myself at times, thrashed about like whales abandoned in a desert. Slowly though, with our partners, we began to mould and craft the new world of joint working and all this, for a time, left Police Chief Officers light years behind.

I could write a thesis on the trials, tribulations and successes of partnership working but that is not for these pages. What is more relevant here is the difficulty experienced in freeing up more police resources to contribute to the new joint attack on crime and disorder. The budget managed by Police Divisional Commanders was almost all comprised of the salary costs of the staff who worked for them. The remainder was the running costs of buildings and vehicles with very little left for anything else.

The Council who was now contributing to the war on crime and disorder wanted to see more police money going into the new team working. Basically, they wanted to see more police officers on the street, a contribution towards the accommodation for the personnel who would work in the new teams and also a share in the hosting of the many meetings which were now taking place.

We had recently conducted a survey of our constables' working days. At one time such exercises were known as 'Time and Motion Studies' and under that title they had caused considerable unrest among the Trade Unions of the United Kingdom. The Police Service is not allowed to have a Trade Union, but it does have a staff association which is called the Police Federation and that body disliked these studies just as much as the Unions.

However, the survey we conducted was as much use to the Federation as it was to management. The conclusion was that police patrol car drivers had very little spare time. In fact, they rushed from job to job most of the time and seldom got out of their cars when they were not dealing with incidents. The public had told us that for years, they used words like, "We never see a Bobby anymore", or "Where are the coppers when you need them?"

A small number of officers, in my Force called 'Area Officers', did walk when on duty, but if I am honest, they were regularly taken away from their basic duties to provide cover on the cars when they were not staffed. Slowly it dawned on me that the only way I could free up resources to contribute to the new partnership working was to change the shift pattern.

Officers wanted a changed working pattern. The Fire Service worked ten- or twelve-hour shifts and our constables saw the greater number of days off that Fire personnel had. For me there might be another advantage. By putting everyone on ten or twelve hour shifts the officers could work eight hours in cars and then spend the remaining hours working on community projects. It might just work.

I now have to digress. It was around this time I was told I was to be interviewed to see if my new job would become permanent. It came and went and yes, I was successful. It was a terrible experience at the time. I did not perform very well. I was too involved in the reality of the job and not easily able to sit back and talk about my vision for the role. I spent much of the interview with my eyes wandering about the ceiling as if searching for inspiration. I was informed that that had been noticed when I was given 'feedback' after the results had come out.

The trauma of going through a selection process when I had been doing the job for several months was quickly forgotten. However, something happened that remains with me to this day and changed a lot of things then and in the future. I have already mentioned the number of times I found myself driving the forty or so miles each way to and from work. Well, in winter it was worse and the country roads at night could be terrible when you felt tired and just wanted to get home.

One evening I was within seven or eight miles away from arriving home. It was absolutely pouring down with rain. The road was covered in water and headlamps reflected from the wet surface with a hypnotic type of effect. Traffic was fairly heavy in both directions though I was trying to keep a safe distance between myself and the car in front. Suddenly, a red car emerged from a road to the left and I braked immediately. However, the vehicle now in front of me was not turning in either direction it just drove across my path presenting its side like a metal wall in front of me. I swerved round it on the wrong side of the road, and I was braking as I did so and suddenly felt a massive bang to the back of my car and I was shunted forward towards oncoming cars. I managed to get back onto the correct side of the road avoiding a frontal collision. The vehicle that had run into the back of me also managed to return to the correct side of the road,

I staggered out of my car and stood gasping in the night air to clear my head. The 'driver' of the red car that had caused this chaos got out and came to me. If I expected an apology, I was wrong because I can remember her words now as clearly as then.

"You rich bastards in your posh cars make me sick. I suppose you'll say it was my fault and I've got no licence."

Rather than exploding with anger the drivers' response left me speechless and I staggered off to the car that had run into the back of me. The driver of that vehicle was a young mother with two small children strapped into child seats. I helped her push her car into a safer position and we exchanged names and addresses. I think my legs buckled at that stage and I can remember very little afterwards. I cannot remember speaking to an officer at the scene of the accident or afterwards at home, I cannot remember how I got to work the following day, though I assume it must have been a courtesy car.

I know I did not want to drive that road two or three times a day at night, in all weathers and in winter. I talked about it with my wife, and we decided to move house again. We did not want to leave the village we had settled in, and it was a mistake to do so. I could have bought a flat in the urban centre of my new Division and kept the village house for days off or when I got posted back to that part of the world. However, retrospect is a wonderful power which, like most people, I never really benefited from!

Then, as we searched for a new home and waited for the village property to sell, the 'Limp Chief' retired. One day he was there and the next gone. Unlike most Chief Officers he did not take employment in a high-profile post for a second career, nor did he make any impact in the voluntary sector or social life of the Force. He just disappeared. If you were to know exactly who he was and look him up on the internet you will find hardly a mention of him and yet there is more about Chiefs from the Victorian era. It seems strange but I must admit that at the time I was just pleased to see the back of him. He had done me no favours in his years in charge of our Force.

Very soon after the departure of the 'Limp Chief' I had a visitor form the past. A character, who had been nicknamed Damien when we both attended the Police Special Course, had risen to the rank of Deputy Chief Constable and he had decided to apply for the Chiefs' vacancy in my Force.

We met in my office at Divisional Headquarters, and I spent most of the time trying to work out what he had that I obviously did not. He was about to become a Chief Constable and I was a newly promoted Chief Superintendent. He had a broad northern accent, was not particularly imposing from a physical point of view and his hair was thinning to the point of extinction. However, when I look back at what he did achieve in the Police Service it is amazing that our Police Authority failed to select him at the interview which took place soon after his visit with me.

Not many years later after being the Chief Constable of another northern Force he became the Commissioner of the Metropolitan Police Force. His nickname there was "Tango" as he had a permanent tan from holidays abroad. We hardly ever met again in the twenty some years that has passed since the day in my office. However, for me he was one of the good guys. When I retired and he was still serving he sent me a Metropolitan helmet as a memento, and he left me wondering. Had he become our Chief at that time would my career have blossomed under an old friend whom I trusted. We shall never know.

The man who did become our new Chief Constable was a man of integrity, honesty and courage. His views on Policing were very similar to mine, or mine were very similar to his as he had been a police officer for a lot longer than me and he had walked the walk of local policing a lot longer than I had. He was not completely new to us. He had been a Chief Superintendent in our Force before leaving to become Assistant Chief Constable of a Force not that far away. Two years before the departure of the Limp Chief he had returned as our Deputy Chief and now slipped into the Chiefs' job like he had always been there.

Digression over. We now return to my proposal to allow a change of working hours at my Division. The new Chief was very reluctant to allow one Division to make a change while the others remained on the traditional pattern. I sold the initiative as an experiment with a full evaluation report provided to Strategy Team in six months. It looked like a green light was about to be forthcoming. Then the Federation threw a spanner into the works by pointing out that every member of my staff had to agree to the change if it were to be implemented. I felt sure that among two hundred and fifty police officers one would dig their heels in as a protest, but no one did. The change could take place.

Well, I will not claim that the change went without a hitch. It did not. To begin with the main station was regularly full of officers doing paperwork and catching up on interviews. It proved extremely difficult to get the 'free time' translated into officers on the street solving problems. However, strong supervision slowly emptied the police station, and the public did start to notice a difference in the police presence on the streets.

We were into the third month of the experiment and progressing fairly well when Armageddon fell on all four Divisions. Each Commander received a message telling us that we should attend a meeting at Force Headquarters. There was no detail about the meeting, we were merely informed that we had to be there in person with no deputies acceptable. It was a mystery, and someone suggested that we were all to be removed from our posts with the new Chief wanting a clean sweep before he started his new regime.

The following morning, we were greeted at the door of Force Headquarters and escorted to a classroom on the top floor of the building. The next hour was then spent speculating about the subject we would soon be discussing. The waiting made things worse as, I am sure, did the vast quantity of coffee we consumed.

After what seemed an eternity, the Chief entered the room followed by his Deputy, the Detective Chief Superintendent and my predecessor, the 'Chinless Wonder', in his new role as head of Corporate Services Department. All four took a place behind a table at one end of the room and we were invited to take seats at the other side.

Most of what followed is blurred in my memory by the shock of what we were told and the impact that the meeting had on us over the coming days, weeks and months. My recollection is that the Deputy did most of the talking that morning. He had clearly come to deliver a message that the three of them had agreed upon prior to our being called in.

"The Chief wants to introduce Local Policing Teams across the Force area. Things are going to change dramatically. This is going to happen quickly, and we want you to introduce them."

Initially, I felt excited and invigorated by what I had just heard. The other three looked even more shocked than I felt. Surely this news was a vindication of what I had already started in my Division and had pursued since the days I worked as a sector commander. This initial feeling of euphoria quickly dissipated as the 'Chinless Wonder' interposed.

"This will be completely new. James has created a bastardised hybrid at his Division. That is not the vision we have in mind...." The rest of what he said floated over my head. I had changed the shift pattern after convincing the staff to support me and now only halfway into the experiment everything was to be totally changed again. Further, I felt that I would look like a fool in the eyes of our partners as they had changed their working patterns to fit in with what I had negotiated.

Those facing us with the Chief had rehearsed the whole meeting. In our shocked state the Divisional Commanders were outmanoeuvred at every turn and question. In essence we were being asked to manage a revolution in Policing. There would be no more CID Department on Division, there would be no Traffic Department and we would need a whole lot more Police buildings.

Each Local Policing Team would have its' own base in the community it served. The LPT would have officers with investigative skills and road policing skills attached to them, but these would be supervised by the sergeants and inspectors running the whole team. I could see the logic of this. To deliver local policing in the communities we serve more resources were needed. I had tried to free up more resources by using mine more efficiently with a different shift pattern. The new Chief was putting all the Forces' operational resources into LPTs' so those with special skills could be seen on communities and help spread those skills among all team members.

We were told to go away and discuss with our management teams how many LPT's we would need to deliver the model. They would tell us what staff we would acquire from the break-up of Headquarters Departments. We were also tasked with establishing where the LPTs' would be based. We were told to consider existing Police buildings, Council buildings, Shopping Centres and possibly new build on brown field sites. We were given a week to do this preliminary work before the next 'get together' at Force Headquarters.

I think it was myself who asked if the vision was set out in a paper that we could see. The answer was that we would need to wait a while for that to be available. I am still waiting twenty years after that initial meeting took place and so, as far as I am aware, are those who were my colleagues at that time.

Now let me confuse you for a minute or two. Two years after the introduction of LPTs' I attended a course at the Police Staff College, Bramshill. When I arrived there, I noticed that my Force were making a presentation to the Senior Command Course. I was informed by a friend who attended 'our' presentation that those present had been impressed by the work that had been done to introduce LPTs.' Particularly the Project Management and Consultation phases of the project were seen as being excellent. I can only assume that the presentation was based on fantasy and the history had been written after the event by the 'winners' (the Chiefs' Team) because I never saw a single document or any sort of plan, not even one on the proverbial 'fag packet'. The Divisional Commanders were given a vision and our products were accepted or rejected as we submitted them.

At Division I was bombarded with questions, criticism and prophesies of doom; there was very little in the way of positive contributions. However, when I did return to Force Headquarters, a week after the first meeting, I did have a plan that I felt might work. Once again, the shock tactics of the Chief Officers swung into motion. I had gone to this second meeting with a proposal for there to be four LPTs' on my Division; my argument would have been that four would be far enough to stretch my resources without spreading them too thinly. I was told that my Division would have six LPTs' based on six identifiable communities. I guessed immediately that the 'Chinless Wonder' had been dabbling since the last meeting. I could have come up with twelve communities or more but eventually we would run out of enough officers to have one on each team!

I really tried to persuade the Chief Officers that four would be the ideal number. I met a brick wall. "What part of six do you not understand?"

From this point I think all the Divisional Commanders realized that this was not a consultative meeting in which negotiation had any role whatsoever. I returned to my Division and came up with the boundaries for the six LPTs'. My management team and I found six bases from which the LPTs' could work, although some would need new building on land that had been identified as available. We also started to divide the existing staff up and allocating them to the as yet none existent LPTs'.

It is often claimed in organisations that morale has reached rock bottom, but seldom have I experienced such a unanimous conviction that this was the case as it did at that time. My belief in local policing was tested to the limit. There were some days when we could not put a police car on the motorway because we could not double crew such a car (two officers were required in cars on the motorway because of health and safety reasons in the event of a major collision or incident). There were occasions when we could not find an officer with investigative skills in the whole Division, when at one time we had a team of twenty available. The experimental shift pattern which had supported my plans for local policing created an enormous strain on resources in LPTs' and it became difficult for officers to take time off at short notice.

The idea of having policing teams in communities was based on the belief that we would be more accessible by the public. However, the master plan of Chief Officers had not included any staff to receive the public in our new bases. The result was either keeping an officer off the streets or locking the base up so the public had nowhere to go. The problems just grew and grew while local management tried to make and mend with 'vinegar and brown paper'.

While all this was going on criminals did not have a holiday until we sorted things out. Incidents took place at the most inconvenient of times and the number of partnership meetings seemed to grow and grow. Also, in my early policing days, I had often had problems with animals when I was at work, and it seemed like they were still pursuing me.

One group of officers who seemed largely unaffected by the recent changes were the dog handlers. They still trained their dogs, drove to incidents in their vans and usually did an excellent job. Then, one day, when I was about to drive to Force Headquarters and beat seven bells out of the 'Chinless Wonder,' I received a phone call from the Force Solicitor. He in turn had received a letter from a football team, based on my Division, alleging that some of their players had been attacked by one of our police dogs.

I had not heard about this. Probably some caring individual had thought that I had enough on at the moment but the problem would not go away. The dog handler had been training his dog in a derelict building one sunny, Sunday morning when the dog decided it had had enough. The dog exited the building, jumped a wall and started to chase the ball that was being kicked by two football teams. Attempts to deter the dog caused the referee to be bitten and several items of kit had been torn by the rampaging canine.

The match was called off and both teams adjourned to a local pub where they no doubt compared injuries and vented their wrath on the modern police service. I wanted to contact the team managers and the referee, but the solicitor was adamant that everything went through him. In one sense this lifted the problem from me but the letters that arrived seemed very personal, particularly the one from the FA which questioned my ability as a "manager of men" and made no adverse comment about my handling of animals!

While the correspondence about the dog floated backwards and forwards a horse decided to get involved in the mayhem that was taking over the Division. Noel Edmunds still has slots as a presenter on national radio but at that time he seemed to be on the television every day of the week. His popularity seemed to have no bounds, even when he started performing with what looked like a large pink sausage called 'Mr. Blobby'. Indeed 'Mr. Blobby' became an icon in his own right and I should have been impressed when it was decided that he should attend an event in our main urban area.

The crowds were much larger than the Council had thought, and hundreds packed into the narrow main shopping street. There a police horse, quietly engaged in a day out window shopping, was suddenly alarmed by this large pink object bouncing around him in a strange way. The horse should have been used to this sort of thing as they had often remained calm when football hooligans stubbed their cigarettes out on them. Mr. Blobby was an insult too far and the horse kicked out with its back legs.

Mr. Blobby was uninjured but sadly a small boy had been kicked fully in the mouth. It required a trip to the local hospital where he was detained for some time. Several letters were sent to the Force Solicitor, and he now had two files relating to my Division. Both files had brown card covers and a piece of red ribbon round them, one was entitled "DOG", the other, not surprisingly, "HORSE."

If one child had been quite badly injured at a Council event then a whole class was nearly traumatized at a Council facility. I was yet again involved in this but fortunately little came of what could have been a major incident.

One morning I had gone to work early and was ploughing through the pile of paperwork on my desk when I received a phone call from a detective. I was informed that we may have a murder on our hands but there were strange circumstances surrounding the deceased. The body was currently at the Council Swimming Pool, and I was asked if I could attend.

As I arrived, a School Bus was unloading its' passengers outside the Swimming Pool. My only positive contribution to this incident was to ask the accompanying teacher to take her pupils to school instead of into the swimming lesson. There was no fuss and as the bus departed, I entered the Pool Building and was immediately accosted by the pool attendant. He had found a naked body floating face down in the pool and he knew the body had not been there when he closed the pool the evening before.

I could draw this out but will put readers out of their misery. It transpired that someone else had a key to the Swimming Pool and the possessor of the key was a local councillor and head of the Pakistani Welfare Association. That individual was responsible for collecting funds for the burial of his members and on occasions repatriating deceased to Pakistan. It transpired that his Association, which had hired the pool, did not make the booking for the purpose of swimming. The purpose was for the ritual washing of the bodies of the deceased and on this occasion one of the bodies was left behind.

I was relieved that the pool attendant had inspected the pool before the children had been allowed in. If they had then the Councils' Legal Department would have been receiving the sort of letters ours was. The booking was cancelled, and the Association had to make other arrangements for their body washing activities. Fortunately, this whole event never attracted the publicity that Mr. Blobby had done.

While the dramatic intervention of animals in my career ended with the horse incident I was once kept waiting by a lorry load of fish. I had arranged a meeting with the leaders and representatives of the many ethnic minorities which lived in my Division. In order to get a good attendance, I had set the date for a Sunday morning. I was there half an hour early to set everything up, but another half hour later there was only myself and two Somali men.

I had several cups of tea with my two guests and an hour later I was about to call it a day when I received a message from the Police Station Reception. My guests had arrived. There were thirty-six of them in total and all of them had either a carrier bag or a newspaper package with them. The day I had chosen for the meeting was the day that the fish lorry from Bangladesh arrived and it had been late.

The meeting, once everyone had arrived, went on and on. It was amicable but I am not certain we achieved an awful lot. It was when the time came to draw things to an end that the interesting bit really started. Several of the attendees wanted to talk to me in private and I did try to facilitate this to a limited extent. It became obvious that the communities were not as homogenous as they had once appeared to me.

My first one to one opened a real bag of warms. I was informed that the head of a local charity was dishonestly appropriating funds for his own use. While the second chat claimed that the provider of the first information was a "bad man and a crook." It went on in that mode with allegation after allegation pouring out and most of them having their roots in old grudges that went back years.

Shortly after that meeting I received evidence that the Imam of a local mosque had been forcing a young girl to have sex with him. Best practice suggested that we should inform the community leaders that we were about to arrest one of their religious leaders. We did everything by the book and the following morning when we attended at the mosque, we found that the Imam was no longer to be found. Indeed, by that time he was already safe in Pakistan. My officers were frustrated and annoyed by what they saw as a system designed to undermine their efforts. There were suggestions that we had soft pedalled in the face of Islam, and it did set relationships back some way.

I can, however, provide an element of balance here. I have already set out in these pages just how committed I was to partnership working. I spent half a day a week in the office of the Chief Executive of the local Council. It was, therefore, only courteous that I forewarned him that we were about to arrest the

Leader of the Council as he arrived at his office in the Council Building. (To avoid confusion; the Chief Executive is a paid employee of the Council while the Leader is an elected politician who leads the majority party in the Council).

In this case the person to be arrested was alleged to be part of a paedophile ring and the evidence was particularly strong. As my officers arrived at the Council Building so did members of the local and national media. Clearly someone had tipped off the journalists about the arrest. The Council solicitor was also present, and a quiet arrest had become a high profile and widely talked about event.

Why did we make the arrest at the man's place of work? Well, that had been out of human consideration. The Council Leader lived with is elderly mother and it was felt that the upset to her would be the greater harm than arresting him at work. Perhaps we will always be "Damned if you do and Damned if you don't." What I will say is that that man was found guilty and imprisoned. He arrived in our cells a smart, upright man and a figure of authority. Later the next day, when I went to review the extension of his custody in our cells, he was a shabby little man who smelled of cheap aftershave and sweat. He threatened to end my career if he was not immediately released. Perhaps he did, as I never rose any higher in rank, but his career was certainly over and there would be no way to hold his head high in the local community on his release.

CHAPTER FIFTEEN

BANG

One Bank Holiday the sun was shining in a blue sky, and it was one of those days when you felt good to be alive. I decided to take my wife and son to a rugby match, some three or four miles, as the birds would fly, from my home. My son loved our trips to rugby matches and he was excited long before we set off from home.

Unusually we had to queue at the turnstiles and that probably saved the price of three admissions. As we waited to gain entry I heard a loud noise, more of a thud than a bang, and my immediate thought was that a bomb had gone off. Looking to the south, from where we were standing, I saw a huge column of orange and yellow flame topped by a plume of black smoke. I knew straight away that I would be called out and my phone was ringing as we got back to our car which was parked near the rugby ground. The explosion had taken place at an oil refinery not far from our home and I was required to make my way to the scene immediately.

Having dropped my family at home en route to the refinery. I arrived there some thirty minutes after the explosion. After all these years, I cannot remember exactly how many fire engines there were battling to cope with the wall of flames. I do remember seeing the fire officers milling around, with the fire making them look like ants compared with it.

The senior Fire Officers at the scene were very close to the fire. They were busy making real time decisions as the circumstances changed, so it was difficult to establish good communications with them. The Police base was some way distant from the refinery as we were to be an overall command centre and location to which resources would report on arrival.

We quickly closed all the roads that led to the refinery and the neighbouring village. Then there was a strange stillness, a feeling of peace and tranquillity during which we actually had nothing to do. The Police roll is to coordinate all resources in incidents like this and to be ready to evacuate local residents if the circumstances required it.

At this stage no one had used the magic term, 'Major Incident'. If anyone had done that then the whole emergency command structure would spring into being. Police Chief Officers, together with the Fire and Ambulance Chiefs, the Chief Executive of the local Council, Emergency Planners and a host of other senior personnel with a roll to play in restoring normality. That group of people would be designated 'Gold Command' and they would be based at Police Force Headquarters which could be miles away from any event. My base would, after the magic words, have become the 'Silver Command' and those with specific jobs, near the site of the disaster, would be entitled 'Bronze Command'.

The officer in charge of the Police Command and Control Centre receiving the initial alert of the explosion could have used the magic words at that stage. Similarly, the Fire Officer in command of all those resources at the scene could have declared the incident a Major Incident. Finally, I had the authority to set the wheels in motion and I was in a difficult position.

Two individuals had had the opportunity to declare Major Incident status but, for whatever reason, they had not done so. Now I would effectively be overriding their earlier decisions if I decided to raise the profile of the incident. At this time the flames appeared to be subsiding, but the Fire Service would not state that they had the fire under control.

One of my staff had made contact with a member of the site management and I was being told that no one had been injured on the site of the refinery. Further, there were no reports of injury to any members of the public and, perhaps most significantly, the smoke from the fire was not believed to be toxic.

At this point I received a phone call from the Chief Officer who would have taken command of Gold Command if the magic words were used. We discussed the situation at length and, on the information I passed to him, it was decided that

Gold would not be established at that time. So, my team and I waited, the police staff on the roadblocks waited and, most importantly, local residents waited. Meanwhile the Fire Officers continued to risk their lives to put the fire out and the management of the refinery were no doubt in panic as they anticipated the inquiry that would inevitably follow an event of this nature.

It was during the 'waiting time' that I realised just how little we knew in my command centre. The management of the refinery were largely to blame for the gaps in our information. It transpired that at one stage no one knew how many people were actually on the site and the report of there being no injuries was more of an optimistic guess at that stage. Further, as no one from the refinery management team ever attended at my command centre we were never informed what steps they had taken regarding the local population of the neighbourhood. We were informed that the management had alerted the local residents and they would also sound a siren when normality was restored.

Several hours later the facts, that had coloured my earlier decision making, were proven to have been fairly accurate. There had been no serious injuries to anyone working on the site and thankfully neither had there been to local residents. People on and off the site had been thrown over by the shock of the explosion but how no one died is little short of a miracle.

The fact that the explosion took place on a Bank Holiday was perhaps the most significant cause in no one dying. The administrative staff were all away from work on that day and their usual working stations were swept with shards of hurtling broken glass. Metal was incinerated, melted, torn and twisted into unreal shapes. Pieces of structure were hurled high into the air and rained down on the periphery road and adjacent properties. Windows were shattered in many local houses.

I took the roadblocks off several hours after I arrived at the scene, and I stood down some of the police staff shortly thereafter. I left a van load of officers to secure the site until the following day (as the refinery would remain a potential crime scene until there had been a proper investigation) and I also asked them to be highly visible to the local residents. We made contact with the local council and road clearing began almost immediately.

By the following morning I had a letter from the Chief Officer whom I had spoken to from the incident. I was impressed by how quickly he had sent that message; it thanked my staff and I for the efficient way with which we had responded and dealt with the incident. We should all have had a party, but I was about to feel excluded from the festivities.

I was at work the following morning but feeling a bit lethargic and less enthusiastic than usual. By lunchtime I had received an invitation to an evening meeting at the village hall adjacent to the refinery. My first reaction was that the meeting was being called by the Council who were now responding twenty-four hours late. My partnership head said I should attend but my self-interest head said that this was a meeting I did not need after the trauma of the previous day. I decided that I would have the evening at home and asked my secretary to tender my apologies to the meeting.

Then, less than an hour later, I received a phone call from a local Member of Parliament. She "demanded" my attendance and made it clear that if I chose to absent myself there would be a complaint to the "highest authority". It was explained that the meeting was to provide reassurance to the local residents, and it was this rather than the bullying tone of the MP that resulted in my attending.

I informed my Chief Officer that I was going, and he reminded me of the limitations on what I could say. There would most likely be an inquiry into the incident and my opinions and conjecture should be reserved until presented at any hearing.

If I did not expect a pat on the back for what had been achieved the previous day, I certainly did not expect what did happen. As I drove to the Village Hall on a dark, damp evening I felt quite calm, reassured by what I thought had been a job well done. Then as I parked near the Hall, I realized immediately that this was not to be the low-profile event that I had been promised. There were at least three television company crews, several national journalists and a host of reporters from the local papers.

The Council and the Fire Service had turned out in force, as had the company running the refinery. I noticed that some of the company representatives, who all seemed to be wearing the same style and colour of suits, seemed to be circulating among the residents with what looked like cheque books.

My 'buddies' from the Crime and Disorder Partnership seemed reluctant to talk to me and I seemed to be the only person not offered a coffee. To be accurate, the representatives of each body tended to cluster with their own and I was by myself. Strength in numbers appeared to be the order of the day and I had obviously got that wrong.

A local councillor opened the meeting with an audience that filled every bit of space available, some were sat on window ledges and others stood on chair seats at the back of the room. He thanked the Fire Brigade, commented on the bravery of the local residents and even complimented the speed of response by the company. Then he said he was a little disappointed by the Police and sat down.

The MP who had rung me, then decided that she must address this congregation of potential voters. She was a pale skinned, red headed, fire brand of a woman. I did not like her before the meeting, and I detested her after it. The woman was a sneak. Every MP that I worked with, other than her, worked closely with representatives of local agencies. So, if an MP got a complaint about a policing issue in my area, they would invite me to respond before taking any other action on the matter. This MP never wrote to me once nor had she ever rung me before she the call to ensure my attendance at the Village Hall. Her method was to go straight to the Chief Constable or write a disparaging letter to the Home Secretary.

Her short speech followed the direction provided by the Councilor, then she announced that I hadn't really wanted to be there that evening, but she had insisted. She rounded up by thanking the company for providing so many local jobs in her constituency.

Now, by this point I realized that I was sitting alone at one end of the 'top table'. All those who had been involved in the events of the previous day, plus the Council, were sat at the other end.

Then I was asked if I wished to 'defend' my position. I was stunned and annoyed. I said that I did not have a position, I had merely been part of a positive response to an event which took place on private premises. I also stressed that I did not think that there was anything to defend.

The Councillor who had opened the meeting now leaped to his feet. It transpired that his grumble stemmed from the fact that my staff did not use a loud hailer to notify residents that they were safe to come out of their houses. I had left a unit of eight officers in the village to provide reassurance and I had heard the coverage of the incident on the local radio station. I could also have mentioned one key point at his stage. The refinery like all similar sites in the UK were at that time subject of the Control of Major Accident and Hazard Regulations and they were required to have an 'off site plan' that would cover the issues I had just been asked about. Sadly, the plan was not in place. The COMAH regulations had only just come into force and previously plants had been covered by the Control of Industrial Major Accidents and Hazards Regulations (CIMAH). The off-site plans were prepared by emergency planners who worked for the Council. The company had to supply information to the Council. They had done so but as yet there was no new plan in place.

On the day of the explosion then there was no new plan, no one could find the old plan and the company would send no one to my control point. We did the best we could and if I mentioned the position regarding the plan then clearly the emphasis should have shifted to others at the meeting. I did not feel that I could do this as the inquiry would look into issues such as that.

After the meeting in the Village Hall, I did ask my own Chief Officers to take up the question of communication with the Fire Service, the Council and the company. To the best of my knowledge this never happened. I also felt that I had learned lessons which would help in the training programme for our major incident commanders. I had, after all, commanded what the inquiry later referred to as "the most serious chemical incident in GB since 1974".

I never gained any official recognition for the police input on the day of the explosion, nor did I ever pass the learning onto any other police officer. In retrospect I think it was easier to brush the whole thing under the carpet because it was never declared a Major Incident and the commander was not a Chief Officer. A good number of Chief Officers have received awards for less than I did on that day but, hey ho, life went on. My nightmares related more to the meeting than the flames, the bangs and the twisted metal.

However, nightmares were to come closer to home not once but three times. The first nightmare occurred when we returned to our house after a holiday in foreign parts. As we drove through the gate at the front of our property my wife suddenly realized that her car was missing. In our house there was a note from officers at my own Division, it informed me that they had secured my house after it had been burgled and they required a statement. This was an experience from the other end of the spectrum of criminality to that I which I was more used to.

The 'job' on our house had been a professional one. The burglars had removed a window from the conservatory, searched the house for keys, loaded my wife's car with goods stolen from the house and they had then locked the door on leaving. The car, a nice Mazda sports coupe, was found burned out some three miles from our house.

My wife tried to get a courtesy car from her insurers, but their words have remained with us over the years.

"You can have a courtesy car if your insured vehicle has been removed to a place of restoration or repair."

Well, my wife's car was a heap of burned and rusty metal that would never again travel under its own power. The car was a total write off but that meant that no courtesy car could be provided. It seemed crazy to me then and it still does now. Six months later, having fitted a state-of-the-art alarm in the interim, we were burgled again. This time we were asleep in the house when the burglars entered through a garage window. They took the stolen goods away this time on a wooden panel that they had removed from the fence at the bottom of our garden. The insurers struck again and dear reader, just out of interest, you cannot claim if you ever have an electric generator stolen from your house. They argued that a generator is not a normal household item!

This time the burglars were caught but that brought no sort of closure for me. Two of those arrested were given Drugs Treatment Orders when they appeared in court and the third was given a Conditional Discharge. Further, the two who were given Drugs Orders had a requirement to attend at my Police Headquarters for their daily methadone. I saw them queueing up at an office right under mine and one of them used to smile at me. At that time, I felt a little like the Detective Chief Inspector in the urinals, but I bit my tongue and soldiered on.

Some sort of closure did come several months later. As I took our dog for a walk, a small motorcycle came screaming towards me. Following, a short distance behind, came a police patrol car with its blue lights flashing. I was about to leap from the footpath into an adjacent garden when the motorcycle veered across the road, jolted as it hit a 'sleeping policeman' (speed bump) and unseated the three young men who had been riding on it. They lay in the roadway, barely moving and then I heard them laughing, deep, belly laughs. They were out of their minds on some substance or other and seemed to enjoy lying on the road.

I recognized the three as those who had burgled our house. One of them was easily recognisable with a face that could not be forgotten. He had a nose squashed across his face and he also possessed a Neanderthal forehead and prominent eye orbs. I will always remember him, and I am fairly sure, if he remembers anything, he will remember me or more accurately our dog. As he lay in the road our dog cocked its' leg up and peed on the burglar.

It transpired that the motorcycle had been stolen, all of them admitted to not having a driving licence and it emerged that they had been paying a friend to provide the urine samples that enabled them to comply with their Drugs Treatment Orders. Two of them received a term in prison but I gained little satisfaction from that.

Our third burglary failed to gain the culprits anything. An alarm, fitted in the garage, activated and they fled into the night. For me, thereafter, as I sat in the conservatory looking out into the night, I could imagine faces lurking in the dark edges of the garden. As you get older the faces just seem nearer and clearer. For my grandmother they certainly did as she was burgled several times.

Eventually she had bars put up at all the windows in her bungalow and lived like a prisoner in her own home. Then one evening two burglars arrived with a hydraulic jack which they used to force the bars apart. They then broke a window and climbed in over my grandmother who lay there terrified in her bed. They spent quite some time in the bungalow before leaving with almost everything that was worth anything and a host of sentiment and memories went with it.

As a policeman you cannot dwell too much on what you see, experience or hear from those that did. There was one meeting that often chilled me to the bone. That was the Multi Agency Public Protection meeting.

There are offenders living in our communities who really belong in crime fiction. These people have the most perverse sexual deviances, almost uncontrollable violent urges and individuals who share no common feelings of empathy with the majority of us human beings. These people are interested solely in themselves and the satisfaction of their basic drives.

In an effort to control this small but frightening minority all the agencies put their rivalries and work pressures aside to focus on how to cope with them. The Council Leader who I mentioned earlier would fall into this category. Driven by urges beyond his control that led him to defile young children, he moved in a network of like thinkers. As quickly as one of them is plucked from their disgusting lifestyle they are replicated or replaced in the network, and it goes on. They are often the people who their communities would least expect and are all the more dangerous because of that.

Most of the readers of this chapter will have heard of the Sex Offenders Register in which those who have committed a sexual offence are listed and required to comply with certain conditions. Some of those on the Register have to do little other than inform the police where they are living, others must report their movements, while yet others are routinely visited by police officers at their homes and places of work. The problem is that the number of registered offenders rises all the time.

The sixteen-year-old who has sex with his fifteen-year-old girlfriend, through my police colleague mentioned earlier, on to a Police Chief Superintendent who raped his own daughter, to the individual who murdered two young girls and indirectly ended the career of the creator of LPTs'.

My Chief Constable, for most of the time I was Divisional Commander, had joined the Police Service in 1967. It took him eight years to become a sergeant and another five years to achieve inspector rank. His early career did not suggest a highflyer with a top job firmly in his sights, yet in the seven years from 1992 to 1999 he rose from Chief Superintendent to Chief Constable.

This man had helped create the role of Director of Intelligence which saw me promoted to the superintendent rank. He then left our Force to become an Assistant Chief Constable in a neighbouring Force, before returning to us as Deputy Chief Constable when the "Limp Chief" was still in office. He eventually succeeded as Chief Constable in 1999.

As one man was rising dramatically through the police ranks another individual was becoming more active in his life. This second man had been born seven years after the first had joined the Police. An asthma sufferer he had a turbulent time at school, and he was often bullied. Forced to move school on more than one occasion he left full-time education at the earliest possible opportunity. Soon after leaving school, he developed a liking for girls, particularly young ones and he was seen out with thirteen-year-olds when he himself was a good five years or more older than them.

In 1994 our man married after a whirlwind romance, but his marriage did not last long. His new wife soon decided that she preferred his younger brother and moved in with him. The divorce was not granted until 1999 as our Chief Constable finally reached that rank after thirty-two years police service. Even before his divorce our man had fathered a child with a fifteen-year-old girl in 1998. A later inquiry into his behaviour revealed that he had sexual contact with eleven underage girls between 1995 and 2001.

In January 1998 he was charged with burglary, and this followed an earlier charge of rape against an eighteen-year-old. Neither case arrived in court due to a lack of evidence. He moved out of our Force area and then in 2001 applied for the post as a caretaker at a local college. In November, despite his history of sexual contact with minors, he was given the job. His girlfriend also secured a position as a teaching assistant at the local primary school.

Then in August 2002, with our Chief Constable firmly established in post and LPTs' up and, after a fashion, running, the man committed a horrific double murder of two young girls. He was convicted of those crimes in December 2003 and by that time I was no longer a Divisional Commander.

So, it is now time to bring all these strands together and link them to a theme I outlined earlier in these pages. My first job as a superintendent was to create the intelligence structure to take our Force forward. Under my guidance a Force Intelligence Bureau was created with a network of Divisional Intelligence Bureaux. With my right-hand man, we introduced analysts, computerised crime pattern analysis, the creation of intelligence packages to drive police operations and innumerable other new procedures and practices. However, I had failed to get Chief Officers to accept that in attempting to comply with the Data Protection Act we were throwing away pieces of information that would let us down in the future. I tried everything including, you may remember, an implied threat of blackmail!

The situation was a disaster waiting to happen. We had an antique computerized crime information system that had been tinkered with when it should have been replaced. Very few staff understood the working of the original computer and a much smaller group understood the reasons behind the tinkering.

Chief Officers relied on the advice of the Force Solicitors, and I could not persuade them that other Forces seemed to do things rather differently. So, we continued to 'weed' the system by deleting things that had not already resulted in convictions or some other positive recorded action; we deleted far more than we kept. Thus, we threw away much of the background information that would have prevented our man securing employment with young people.

After he was imprisoned a Government Inquiry was commissioned to look into how he came to gain access to children. I remember being called to a 'training session' for those who may be called to give evidence to the Inquiry. I certainly expected to give evidence, as did the inspector who had worked for me in my time in Intelligence. By this time, he had retired on ill health grounds and was not present at the training event.

About twenty-five people attended the 'training'. There were Chief Officers present, but the input was provided by two barristers. We were asked to write down what we thought we would say at the Inquiry and then we were provided with 'advice' as to how we should say it and what we should omit altogether. We were instructed about personal liability, who the Force lawyers were representing and the importance of fully briefing our own lawyers. The majority of those in the audience were terrified by what was said to them and the way in which it was presented. I am sure that the majority would say exactly what was suggested to them.

I was not called before the Inquiry. How was I not? I was there when the system was set up; I had heard the complaints of those trying to work the system and I had passed those on to Chief Officers. Indeed, I had gone beyond the norm in trying to get Chief Officers to take some action. Instead of myself the Director of Intelligence who took over several years after I had left was called to give evidence. He clearly knew the system, but he could not have known the history of how we arrived where we did.

Two detectives visited my retired inspector at his home and said that they had come to take a statement from him. He realized the importance of that statement and he declined to provide it to them. Instead, he visited a solicitor and submitted his typed statement direct to the Inquiry. Years later he told me that he was not called to give evidence and he also insisted that his evidence was not attached to the list of statements published with the Inquiry Report.

I am more than a little uneasy when organisations hold events like our 'training session'. I am certain that an event or series of events will have been held in South Yorkshire after the disaster at Hillsborough. Whatever the real reason behind these events they smack of 'closing shop', 'towing the line', threatening those who step out from 'the battle lines'.

Now, when he commissioned the Inquiry the Home Secretary must have realized that his own head could well have been on the line. For years Forces had argued the Police Service needed a national, shared intelligence system. Instead, the country had a piecemeal, patchwork quilt of systems that did not interconnect and really served no one. The Police National Computer would tell you who was wanted or had been convicted but it contained none of the vast amounts of information that Forces collected as a matter of routine.

Inevitably, when the report of the Inquiry emphasised the failure of the Government, the Home Secretary will have looked for the highest-ranking scapegoat and gone for our Chief Constable. The Chief had not been in post when most of the relevant events had taken place and I am pretty sure that on his arrival as Chief none of his Chief Officers went to him and said, "Hey Chief. We've got a bit of a problem here."

So, put on the spot and called to account, the Chief will have asked for all the old paperwork and advice given to his predecessor and colleagues. That advice will have said, because I know that it did, "we have to delete information because the Data Protection Act says we must."

The Chief should have been safe as houses but now he was told by his legal team, funded by ACPO (his work association), that he could not or should not blame the Data Protection Act or the Information Commissioner who operated under that Act. He was to be the scapegoat it stunk then, and it still stinks now.

The Inquiry Report is just about right in all its two hundred or so pages. It basically says that the intelligence system in our Force was so inefficient that records were destroyed or lost. The failings were said to be endemic and to have continued for many years. It also said that it was "astonishing" that no national intelligence system had been created when it was clearly earmarked as a priority for ten years.

I left the Intelligence Bureau in 1998 and in 1999 the work of my inspector resulted in the amendments to the Force Crime Information system (CIS) which, became known as CIS 2. As a result, a name could be checked through the Nominal Index, however, between 1999 and 2003 there were still staff who had no idea that this could be done. Leadership, resources, and lack of ability are all called into question but all those should not have been dumped on the shoulders of our Chief. The basic problem had festered for years. Who owned the CIS? Who should have made it work and provided the training? Who should have got to grips with the use of it and the issue of deleting information? The system had belonged to the IT Department and searching it was a specialist skill that was beyond police officers, it was operated for the CID, and no one there had any confidence in it, they did not understand it, they knew how much was deleted and they ignored it. The Force Intelligence Bureau realised there was a problem and tried to put things right with a skeleton staff and no support from Chief Officers. The only Chief Officer ever to show any interest in intelligence was the Chief during his time in our Force as a Chief Superintendent.

The Chief did not blame the Data Protection Act as his lawyers had advised. The Inquiry Report was not quite so forgiving and stated that the judiciary had found the Act "an inelegant and cumbersome piece of legislation". The report also said that there was a need for better advice and guidance on the collection, retention, deletion and the use of information. I had tried to say that so many times but then failing to appreciate junior staff is a failing of senior staff in the Police Service. If I had been a consultant there would have been immediate changes but, as it was, I was just a nuisance.

It should also be remembered that there was another Force involved in the horrific double murder that took place. Our man was applying for a job in the area of that other Force. The other Force would have to check with us. There is a question as to whether or not that check was made. If we were asked, then they used a wrong date of birth and only one of the man's aliases.

So, there we are. I am sure that much of the criticism directed at our Force could just as easily have been applied to many other Forces in England and Wales. What must not be overlooked in all this is that two lives were lost, and two families will have been, and probably still are traumatised by what happened. The Police Service let that evil man slip through their hands. I am so sorry!

I wonder if the then Home Secretary still feels sorrow and regret? I have already said he wanted a scapegoat, one big enough to deflect blame from the Government. He called on the Police Authority to suspend our Chief. The Police Authority saw things in a different way as did most of the movers and shakers in our Force area. No one thought a suspension at that time was in the best interest of a Force under immense pressure. The Home Secretary decided to go ahead, and the Police Authority were taken to the High Court. There it was decided that the Home Office had the power to require that a Chief Constable should be suspended.

In the end a deal was done. Our Chief Constable came back but only on the understanding that he would resign and leave several months later. The prodigal son came home to an enormous welcome with applause, cakes and even a little dancing. No one in the Force thought our Chief was responsible and no one forgot those effected by the murders. The celebrations were for a brave man who fell on his sword to save the Force from even greater ignominy and certainly protected some from a fate they probably deserved.

While our Chief was suspended our temporary Chief asked me to apply for a place on the Strategic Command Course which was the gateway to membership of ACPO. I had already decided that I did not want to progress any higher up the career tree. I had a new son, a new house and only five years to the time when I could retire. Further, the rationalist in me could see little chance of anyone from our Force progressing. Our performance had been decimated by the introduction of LPTs' and our intelligence system had just been pilloried we were collectively persona non grata.

Sadly, I didn't handle the invitation all that well. I wrote a report saying that I would not be applying and that I was fed up "playing silly games." There was no need for that last dig at the system and I had opened myself up for attacks from peers and the Chief Officers. From this point I would find out what it felt like to be an outsider.

I had always advised colleagues that survival in the Police Service depended on convincing your immediate supervisor that they had in their power something that you really wanted. In those circumstances the supervisor believed they had you in their hand and at their mercy and if you wanted to get on you did what they said. I had stepped outside the rules of the game and basically undertaken a power game in which Chief Officers have all the artillery. My report had been pointless and, while it was some time before I realised it, the tide of fortune had turned against me.

CHAPTER SIXTEEN

TURNING POINT

My last year as Divisional Commander had settled into more of a routine. The pain and turmoil of creating LPT's had settled into a dull ache. The anguish of forging new working linkages with partner agencies had started to produce results and the bombardment of criticism aimed at everything I had done reduced to a daily trickle.

The Forces' performance was now under the piercing gaze of a number of Government agencies, and this was going to get worse. But for now, we were still at the stage where those 'working on' us were in 'Just Helping' mode and 'take them to the shredder' was still some way off.

I actually employed a firm of consultants to review the performance of my Division. Yes, you already know my views on consultants, but I guess I was buying security.... or I thought I was. The report that emanated from the paid helpers was largely favourable. Set against the upheavals of recent years our performance stood up fairly well against the rest of the Force. Our partnerships were given a five-star rating and a small-scale public opinion poll reported positively on us.

As usual the consultants picked out areas for improvement, particularly in the fields of system testing and quality control (that is, how well do you do what you set out to do and are people provided with a satisfactory product). I was establishing a team to take action on the recommendations, when I was informed by the Chief that I was 'tenured'.

The 'Limp Chief' had established 'tenure' for many police roles such as CID and traffic patrol. It basically meant that you performed a role for five years, or whatever term was set, and then you reverted to basic uniform patrol duties. It was unpopular from the outset; as officers who had just become proficient professionals were then dragged off kicking and shouting to perform duties where their skills were little used. I didn't even realise that there had been a 'tenure' for a Divisional Commanders role.

Well, I had certainly been a Divisional Commander in 'interesting times'. I had never worked less than sixty hours a week and during some periods I was working eighty hours or more between days off. Burn out would have happened if those hours had been continued but, ironically, as just mentioned, things had calmed a little. The stress hit me a few months after I had moved on to other things.

My new job seemed a big one. I had command of all those operational units which remained at Headquarters after the creation of LPT's. So, for example, I had the Helicopter Unit, Operations Planning, Firearms and Firearms Training, the Underwater Search Section etc. It was also likely that the Force Control Room would come under my command bringing with it several hundred staff. Yet in spite of all this I felt like I didn't have a job, not when I compared it to my last role.

There was time to talk to people and get to know what they actually did. I also had the time to thoroughly read all the issue papers that were discussed at Force Meetings. I am fairly certain that this careful perusal of the papers reinforced my reputation as a renegade. I saw problems and alternative solutions in almost every major issue and there were knowing looks and raised eyebrows whenever I spoke. I soon realized that the papers presented on behalf of Chief Officers have, in reality, already been decided upon and they were just there for 'rubber stamping'. Only very rarely did I, or anyone else, secure a positive alteration to any of the endless papers that flowed passed us.

Chief Officers treat members of the Police Authority in just the same way as they did their own senior staff and for me this was a major problem. The Police Authority were part of what was known as the 'Tripartite Arrangement" of Police, Police Authority and Home Secretary. The Police are responsible for day-to-day operational decision making, the Home Secretary provides support, resources and central direction while the Police Authority must ensure that a Police Force is efficient.

The Police Authority in those days was made up of local councillors and independent members. There was a Chair and a Chief Executive. In theory all major expenditure had to be approved by the full Police Authority and they had a say in how the Police performed their duties. I met several new members of the Police Authority and many of them came with an urge to make a big difference in the way the Police operated. However, reality never seemed to work out like that.

The Police Authority members started out as forceful politicians and then they were addressed by the Chief Constable, and they seemed to become hypnotized. They were like rabbits caught in a vehicle's headlamps. They saw themselves as some sort of civilian crime fighting team and they were encouraged to think like that. The Chief Officers rehearsed their presentations, and they managed the Authority members like little children. It was an art form.

Former Police Authority members will tell you what they achieved, how they supported rank and file police officers, what they provided in resources etc. But in reality, they were led by the nose while they sipped tea and ate biscuits in a trance. They provided the buildings for LPT bases before the concept had even been tested, they agreed to swathes of civilianization in the belief that somehow, we put a civilian in a police job and still kept the police officer and incurred no extra cost. It was all like magic and the Chief Officers were the 'wizards' immune from real scrutiny.

With the big in Force meetings the act was the same, but here the majority of those attending had not even read the papers. Those who had made the effort and studied what was written down realised that they were supposed to agree with the recommendations and if they caused a problem their careers could stagnate, or they could be side-lined. It seems sinister but in reality, it was very transparent, and no one really fought it.

With all the conflict going on and more spare time than I was used to, my wife and I bought a house abroad. We had discovered Northern Cyprus as a holiday destination before I even became a Divisional Commander and we had returned at least once a year since our first visit. In 1974 the Turkish army invaded the north of Cyprus largely in order to prevent the genocide of the Turkish Cypriot population. The Greeks fled before the invading army and within weeks a split country had been created with a split capital. A green line divided the country with Turks in the north and Greeks in the south.

The fact that the Turkish army intervened ensured that the international community would not recognize the existence of the north as an autonomous state. Trade embargos were put in place and direct flights were not allowed. Now this is a policing book, and I am not going to get involved in global politics. The significance here is that the north of Cyprus stood still while the south moved on. Mass tourism hit the south of Cyprus with all the major tour operators investing in it in a big way. Two airlines (three for a while) operated between Turkey and the north.

For twenty years the clock stopped in North Cyprus, and we decided to purchase there. It has been largely spoiled since those days, as the olive groves have been bulldozed by the acre to be covered in concrete monstrosities. Mountains of litter seem to be deposited at almost every beauty spot, while cars stand nose to tail emitting fumes that would not meet any emission tests anywhere in the world.

Yet in the days when we decided to settle there it was like a little piece of history preserved in amber, with few cars, very few consumer goods, but unspoiled people and the most excellent, simple foods. Sadly, the working systems carried out in official buildings were a little medieval. A simple piece of paperwork would need signing and stamping in three or four different offices that were often situated in different buildings.

The manual workers would toil all day in incredible heat for what seemed a pittance to us. However, supervision was almost absent though instructions would be followed to the letter.... regardless of implications!

One year a group of workers had been tasked with digging a trench for electric wires. As we sat eating Christmas Dinner with a group of friends, we heard the noise of diggers moving nearer. Fortunately, we looked outside just as the trench reached halfway across our drive. Another hour and the three vehicles parked on our drive would have been marooned for the foreseeable future. Not one worker would have knocked on our door and told us what they were doing, they would just have followed instructions and dug the trench.

My friend had a much more impressive event happen to him. He had a villa built on a piece of land he had bought many years earlier. The villa was finished in record time but unfortunately it had no electric as the builder had not negotiated an electric connection with the power company.

Having waited several weeks for the electric to be connected he went to visit the headquarters of the electric company. After sitting on chairs in three different corridors he finally reached the office of the 'number one man'. There, sat at a desk constructed from highly polished wood and surrounded by chairs made from the most expensive leather available, sat a balding, insignificant little man.

With the help of an interpreter the manager explained that there were no plans to extend the network of electric poles in the area of my friends' house. Eventually the electric would be provided in a series of trenches, but that would be eighteen months to two years in the future.

My friend asked if he could buy an electric pole, and this seemed to transform the meeting. Coffee was called. The merits of the different types of poles were discussed and explained in detail. At last, the discussion arrived at the price required for a pole. The cost was not prohibitive and even the size of the blatant bribe for the manager did not put my friend off. Confident that the solution to the problem was only days away, my friend was sent home to measure the distance from the nearest pole to a location near his house.

The distance was carefully measured, and our intrepid villa owner generously added a meter at each end for the electric engineers to tie the wire to the poles. Having paid in full for the pole, the bribe, the wire and the erecting, he went home to England for a rest.

Some months passed until our villa owner was ready to return to Cyprus. He had received photographs of his villa from the person he paid to look after the property in his absence. In those pictures, light blazed out into the night from wall lights, balcony lights, through open doors and shutters, from the lit pool and even lights wired into the olive trees in the villa's grounds. There was enough light being emitted to have guided a Martian to a safe landing on Earth.

No doubt my friend was properly excited as he drove up to his villa, looking forward to a powered shower after his long flight from England. Then as he swung his car off the roadway ready to enter his drive, he suddenly realized that something was very wrong. There in the middle of his gateway was the pole that he had purchased at great personal expense. No way could anything much broader than a wheelbarrow be got down either side of the pole and certainly a car could not access the property.

The following day, having used all the lights, air conditioning, shower, chilled drinks and food, he drove to the offices of the electric company. He again sat in the three corridors before finally gaining access to the manager. There it was explained that the workers would have laid the wire in a straight line between the last of the poles in the existing network and they put the pole where the wire terminated outside my friends' villa, right in the middle of the gateway. If they had wire, they would use it and my friend had allowed them too much.

Those tasked with erecting the pole had done exactly what they had been asked to do. There was no thought about the implications for access to the property, they had just dug a hole and put a pole up. The solution was amazingly easy. My friend had to pay for the pole to be taken down and put up again in a different location. He also had to pay for the original hole to be filled in and of course a payment to the manager for ensuring that the work was done promptly.

It was not always so easy to laugh at the strange activities of builders when they directly affected you. However, there is something about visiting Cyprus that makes British people behave in a strange way.

We decided to rent our house to friends, relatives and colleagues as a way of funding the maintenance and gardening costs of running the house. It was a short-term project! We had some excellent 'guests' but also a number of people who had little respect for our second home.

We had a bottle of Coke spilled on an expensive Persian rug; suntan oil spilled down a wall and on much of the bedding; candle wax ended up on everything during one visit and there was a long list of items that just disappeared.

One lady complained to our property manager that there was no water at the house. There had been two tons of water when the guest arrived, and it had been explained to her that water in Cyprus was precious. It transpired that the lady had arrived, unpacked and decided to prepare a salad. She had boiled three eggs and then put them under the tap in the kitchen sink to cool them down. An hour and a half later she had drained both water tanks and the mains water was not running at that time.

Another guest, male this time, didn't like hot weather! Why he had decided to visit Cyprus in August where it had an average temperature of over 35C is beyond me. Our manager found him sat outside the house with an electric fan protruding from an open window so that it could blow on him. Every shutter and window in the house were open and the air conditioning was on in every room. We were paying the electric bill while he tried to change the climate of Cyprus!

Our first let had been a memorable one. The house had not long been finished and was basically equipped with consumer goods. We had closed the house down for winter when, out of the blue, my wife received a phone call enquiring about our letting the property.

As the details of the let were concluded my wife asked what name the house was being booked in.

"The name is Tarquin Olivier." Came the reply.

"As in Laurence Olivier?" My wife asked.

"We are those Olivier's." Was the response.

So, we took the booking and fielded enquiries about dry cleaners, restaurants and the like. All the time we worried about whether our little home would be good enough for them and I cringe at what they must have thought.

Our manager had sent a taxi to pick them up at the airport, but the driver had arrived just as the Olivier's were driven off in the Presidential car with a police escort. The cavalcade proceeded to our house which was positioned off an unmade road at the edge of an unfinished building site. There was no street lighting for miles and the nearest neighbour was a goat farmer.

We received a cheque from the Olivier's, and I wish I had kept it. I also wish we could have contacted them to ask about their visit, but we never heard from them again. I understand that the visit was for Tarquin Olivier to work on a film project but again I have no details what it was or whether it was successful.

Now, there is a reason for this unscheduled trip to Cyprus and I will reveal that reason shortly, but I really must share with you an escapade of one of our visitors. That individual was another Chief Superintendent and, as a coincidence, he was my successor at what I will always regard as 'my Division'.

Now, on this trip our guest and his wife decided that they would explore the island and set off for a trip down the Karpas. For those who have no idea where the Karpas is let me be of help to you. If you look at a map of Cyprus, you will see that the outline resembles a frying pan sketched from above. The Karpas is the long narrow bit that resembles the pan handle. It is a region famous as the place where turtles come ashore to lay their eggs, where there are a great number of wild donkeys and for the miles of unspoiled coastline that surround it.

Our visitors had booked into a small hotel overlooking a secluded bay. Just below that hotel was an outdoor dining area and then a number of chalets for guests. Arriving late our intrepid couple had a drink in the bar and then retired to their chalet for the night. A few hours later my colleague got up from bed, summoned by a call of nature, and as he struggled to the toilet, he noticed that the sun was shining, and the sea was sparkling enticingly.

He looked at his watch and saw that it was still only six o' clock. Returning to his bedroom he roused his wife and suggested that they have an early morning swim. She pointed out that they had no swimming costumes with them but when she was told of the time and the fact that they had large bathing towels, she was persuaded.

They quietly crept down to the sea, across the deserted beach and saw no sign of any other guest or staff. Both of them were in their fifties and neither of them would have won a

'Body Beautiful' competition but they frolicked like a couple of teenagers. There was leaping, splashing, breaststroke, backstroke, giggling and generally a good time was had.

Totally relaxed they drifted, naked out of the sea and made their way slowly to their towels. As they did so there was a ripple of applause from the eating area, where upwards of twenty guests were enjoying their breakfasts. I do enjoy telling this story, but can you imagine the embarrassment of a professional couple caught cavorting, totally nude in a moment of high jinks.

The causation of this incident was a technical one or, to be more truthful, a human one. Cyprus is usually two hours ahead of the UK, so six o' clock was in fact eight o' clock and my colleague had failed to change his watch. Hence, the swim took place exactly at that time when most guests of the hotel turn up for breakfast!

My first trip to Cyprus after I had moved on from Divisional Command almost became my last. I had managed to obtain a break from work of three whole weeks. By the end of week one I was no longer even thinking about work. I felt totally relaxed for the first time in several years.

On the last day of the holiday, we had booked a taxi and went for lunch before we started our journey home. I felt absolutely fine until I was halfway through the meal, then I experienced a rushing sensation in my feet, through my calves and then on upwards through the rest of my body. When it stopped, I felt shattered, and my wife said that my eyes were completely red.

An hour later I was in a hospital bed with my blood pressure incredibly high. The doctors kept injecting me in the bottom with something and, whatever it was, it did not do much in bringing the worrying figures down. That night I hid under the sheets as I was dive bombed by hungry mosquitoes and, if I did nod off, I was swiftly woken up by two nurses who thought their role was to laugh at me.

We missed the flight to England and ran up enormous telephone bills phoning work and relatives. Nearly a week later the Doctors did give me permission to fly home. I still felt very strange with regular sessions of palpitations followed by breathlessness. My confidence felt shattered, and I was nervous about leaving our house even if it were only to buy a newspaper.

For a time, no one from work visited me. Then a trickle of visitors began until it eventually worked itself into a steady flow. However, to me, the visits seemed to have an ulterior agenda. The Chief Officers wanted to know if I was going to go back to work or alternatively was, I going to try and secure an early retirement on the grounds of ill health. Where were they coming from? I had a five-year-old son, a mortgage, a minimum of five and a maximum of fourteen years to a normal retirement age (I could retire from the police with thirty years' service, but I could stay on until I was sixty-five.) I could not leave even if I wanted to.

I was, though, absolutely terrified of slipping off the mortal coil. A friend of mine who had had a heart attack described the experience as follows. He said it was like sitting, safe in your own home when suddenly all the walls and windows fall down, and people are looking in at you. I felt exactly like that

I had an angiogram which revealed that there was nothing major wrong with my heart. An ECG (Electro Cardiograph) did show that I had an irregular heartbeat to go with my raised blood pressure. The 'job' sent me to see a Doctor in Leeds and I was very impressed with him. However, it is fair to say that my employers sent everyone there who they thought were fabricating evidence to secure early retirement.

The Doctor induced a panic attack in me by conducting a breathing exercise. He then explained why he thought I was showing all the signs of suffering from post-traumatic stress. It seems that stress creeps into all the cracks in the fabric of your being and when the original cause of the stress is removed your fabric starts to crumble and your body panics.

From that appointment I started to recover. I went back to work three weeks later, though things could never be the same again. I am pretty certain that none of the Chief Officers will have read the report that the Doctor completed on me, however, I am even more certain that some of them will have been convinced I was trying for an early pension. You can see where they were coming from; I had a house abroad and I had told them I did not want to go any further in the Police Service. For them it was a closed case.

Then into the unstable foundation of my working life came another omen of doom. The 'Chinless Wonder' returned to our Force as Deputy Chief Constable. How could our Force hit so many duff notes in recruiting Chief Officers? How could anyone, other than the 'Limp Chief', have ever believed that this individual would bring leadership to the Force in those troubled times? Maybe his previous Force had just sung his praise to get rid of him. If they did, then thanks for nothing. He never progressed any further in the Police Service, he just hung around the Forces' neck like a decaying albatross.

CHAPTER SEVENTEEN

STAFF ISSUES

As I settled into my new job, I realised that I had more time to commit on behalf of my fellow superintendents. I had been secretary of my Force Branch of the Superintendents Association for some years, it was at this time that the opportunity arose to take over as Chair.

In one sense the Secretary did all the work. Whoever held that post was responsible for booking the venue for the meetings and the meals that those attending looked forward to consuming. The secretary also prepared minutes of the meeting, circulated the papers that would be considered and produced the Agenda after consultation with the Chair.

The preparation of written responses to papers considered also fell to the secretary. The Chairs' job was basically that of spokesman and steering issues through the meetings. Most of the time the work required was manageable, though there were occasions when the volume of papers created a problem. The Police Federation, the staff association for ranks up to and including Chief Inspector, had a full-time paid staff and their own offices and clerical support. We were provided with, nothing!

The Federation did have over two thousand staff to look after compared to the twenty or so that we had. However, the issues were much the same and this included discipline issues and legal problems that our members faced. If a constable faced a disciplinary case, then one of the Force Federation staff would look after them and ensure that they had the appropriate level of support. The Superintendents' Association provided legal support from its Headquarters in Surbiton. That seemed at little impersonal, so the Association created a group of 'friends' for any member facing a career threatening situation.

The 'friends' were provided with a training course and were seldom overloaded with cases. They were volunteers and had to fit these duties into their normal work pattern. I once found myself particularly interested in a case covered by one of the 'friends' based in our Force.

Whilst still a Divisional Commander I had applied for a post as a Deputy Chief Constable.! This may surprise you if you have read the more recent pages in this book. However, the circumstances were very different, and the job was certainly different.

The job I applied for was that of Deputy Chief Constable in the Isle of Mann. The island Police Force does not quite conform to the usual pattern in England and Wales where the Home Secretary plays an important part. The Isle of Mann has its own Government and is largely an autonomous entity; so, the Police Force is answerable to the Secretary of Home Affairs of the islands' own Government. By a strange arrangement, although the island Force stands outside the UK Home Office remit, the Isle of Mann submits itself to inspection by H.M Inspectorate of Policing. These anomalies keep you on your toes, don't they?

Another anomaly is that the Chief Constable does not have to have undergone the Strategic Command Course which qualifies officers for ACPO rank. Thus, the Chief Constable, at the time I applied for the Deputy post, was a Chief Superintendent.

So, why would I apply to work for a Chief Superintendent when I already was one?

Well, I will be honest, I liked the idea of wearing the insignia of a Deputy Chief Constable. However, there was much more to it than that. Firstly, the Isle of Mann is a beautiful place, steeped in history and with a great sense of community. Secondly, the job seemed very similar to that of Divisional Commander although the population was forty thousand less than that of my existing command. Thirdly, the thought of bringing my son up in a safe, largely rural environment appealed to me. Fourth, the mercenary in me, the taxation level in the Isle of Mann was far less than in the UK and would equate to a pay rise of around twenty percent.

I was so excited by the job that I almost bounced into my car as I set off for Leeds/Bradford airport, destination Douglas on the Isle of Mann. From that point things started to go downhill. The airport I was to fly from is built on top of a hill and on this day, it was completely fog bound. The weather conditions were such that I struggled to find the airport car park and it was obvious that there would be no flights out for hours.

The airport authorities arranged for me to be taxied to Manchester airport, which was fog free and basking in sunshine. The result of this was that I arrived several hours late for the arranged pick up and I eventually got to my hotel feeling irritated and ill at ease. I sat in the bar trying to calm myself with a succession of lagers; subsequently I slept like a log, before waking the following morning with a dull headache.

Over breakfast I met the other three applicants for the job. There were two superintendents and a Chief Superintendent from a Welsh Force with a vast experience of commanding policing at large football matches. It was a pleasant group, even though there was an underlying rivalry.

We were picked up by a Chief Inspector who took us on a 'whistle stop' tour of the Isle of Mann. Our driver flew along the narrow roads between centres of population and scenic views flashed passed in a blur. We then met the Chief Constable who seemed an amiable enough sort of person and he told us what was to happen over the next two or three days.

I think that was when events started to ring alarm bells. Firstly, the Chief Inspector, who had a little earlier been our driver, was now a fellow applicant for the job. Secondly, a team from a northern Force had been invited to conduct an Assessment Centre as a means of guiding selection. Thirdly, we were about to meet key members of the Government.

The Secretary of State for Home Affairs seemed extremely frosty, and he clearly didn't like the questions I asked about how much control the Police Force had on its' own budget. The reply, in my opinion, was that the Police should get on with policing and let the Government look after the budget. That may well seem common sense to some, but I had been used to managing a budget of millions and if we saved anything we could spend it locally on policing initiatives or new equipment.

The budget of Policing for the Isle of Mann was around fifteen million pounds, however, if anything was leftover at the end of the year it would go back in the 'pot' for redistribution to any area of demand that Government decided on.

I then had one of those moments that I have experienced a number of times in my life. It is a cross between a premonition, feeling the portents of doom, or experiencing that sensation covered by the expression, "someone just walked on my grave". I knew that something was wrong, or at least that things did not feel quite right.

I asked to see the Chief and, fair play to him, he was there in minutes. I told him that I wanted to go home and no longer wished to be part of the process. There followed a heartfelt request for me to stay. The Chief said that he had worked previously with my present Chief, he thought I had an excellent chance of getting the job and there would be problems with numbers at the Assessment Centre if I left.

I left anyway and by the time I reached the airport I thought I had been stupid. Had I just walked out on a fantastic opportunity because I did not like or trust Assessment Centres? I felt like that for several days until I got a phone call from one of the other candidates.

I was told that most of the candidates wished they had left when I did. The proceedings quickly lapsed into farce. To make up numbers at the Assessment Centre a clerical assistant was drafted in. The tests and questions had been fairly routine. The Chief returned at the conclusion of events and quietly told one of the candidates that he could ring his wife because he had got the job. The phone call was made, then things turned sour when out of the blue a member of the Government announced that he had not seen any qualities in the applicants that were not already available in the local candidate. The Chief Inspector was then given the job and all the mainland applicants were shipped back to where they had come from.

My out of body experience had been fully justified, though I regret not having stuck around and created a fuss if things had not worked out differently. We now come to the reason I have been telling you about the Isle of Mann. Within days of the Chief Inspector being promoted he fell out with the Chief

Constable and within a short time of that he was suspended. One of the 'friends' from my Force was allocated to his support team.

I do not know the full details of what happened, though I suspect that there had been suggestions of impropriety by the Chief Inspector. He was cleared of all the allegations made against him. Around the same time as he was being investigated, he made allegations that the Chief had carried out illegal telephone taps. The whole thing became a mess. It seems likely that this debacle was sorted out by the Chief Inspector retiring and being paid nearly a million pounds in compensation. In response he dropped the case against the Chief Constable and life in the Isle of Mann went back to normal.

Quite clearly the 'friends' system worked all round. However, the Government would have been better off financially if they had been more transparent in their recruiting methods. As final comments, I thought the successful candidate was a great guy and I wrote to congratulate him after the announcement of his promotion. Also, it is clear that there can be dark powers moving in even the most outwardly idyllic seeming situations.

For the rest of my career the circumstances at work were far from idyllic. There were moments of elation at temporary successes, but overall work felt like I was shovelling mud up hill. However, I do not need to depress you totally at this stage. I seemed to be developing an understanding with our 'Chief on borrowed time' and once or twice I took the opportunity of sharing my opinion with him about the state of the Force.

It would not have helped to have told the Chief that his LPT's were a load of garbage and that they had effectively destroyed our Force. Firstly, I did not think that everything about LPTs' was bad, but secondly, I could never have attacked a man who I held in such high regard as I did this Chief. For honesty, integrity, guts in testing times and loyalty to his staff I could not fault him.

What I did spend time pedalling to him was my belief that our Force was selling partnership working short. In one or two areas we performed like world beaters but in others we were scarcely on speaking terms. Most significantly, in the partnership arena, our Divisions operated like independent Police Forces and the Chief Officers had no idea what was going on in their name. I once said to the Chief that there could come a day when he went to a meeting and found that he had lost part of his geographical area and that a new Force there now answered to the Chief Executive of the Council. I was tongue in cheek, but it must have rung a few bells.

Several weeks after I last spoke with the Chief I was called into his office and told that I was changing jobs again. I was leaving the Operations Support Command and becoming, wait for it, the Partnership Manager. What on earth was that all about? Well, it must have been me bashing on about a corporate approach to partnership in the Force but what would it involve. Now it was my turn to be caught unaware. Just as the Chief had launched LPTs' without having thought it all out in advance, now I had a job that I had not defined even in my own mind.

Did the Chief create that job because I had been ill? Had I stirred something in him that he could not put his finger on? Whatever the reason behind the creation of the job it no longer exists now and I will leave it to you to decide if I achieved anything.

The first task was to come up with a job description and get that approved by Chief Officers; that was a battle in itself. I began by saying that there should be a 'snapshot' of what partnerships existed in Force, what resources we committed to them, what documents and protocols existed and, if possible, an attempt should be made at costing our input.

I then suggested that all policies and strategies in the partnership and community safety areas should be under the umbrella of the Partnership Manager and finally I stressed the need for the Force to have a library of best practice in the area of local policing.

Slowly but surely the job description was accepted. I had acquired an office at the end of a corridor occupied by Chief Officers, and it was full of reasonable office furniture and equipment. I attended the Force Strategy Meeting and still felt part of the 'top team'. This feeling of comparative wellbeing was to be challenged when I attended the next Chief Officers Meeting with my proposed budget for the Partnership Unit.

Even after all this time I cannot believe that five Chief Officers arrived at a meeting, governed by an agenda, where they had no idea what I was going to do, who I would do it with, where I would do it from, who was going to pay for it and which of them would I report to.

I expected a fight over finance and resources, but it felt like LPTs' all over again. "Go away and come back and tell us...." Only this time I was told that there was no money whatsoever.

Have you ever played 'Ducks and Drakes'? I did as a young boy, skimming flat stones over the local tarn for hour upon hour. I will feel like the stone skimming across the water in the coming pages. Over the coming years I became something of an authority in the area I worked in only to be dumped on the scrap heap of life at a time when I was at my most productive.

In the days immediately after my meeting with Chief Officers I found offices for myself and the staff that I did not have. I came up with an idea whereby each Division funded half a post of a sergeant for my core staff. I discovered that there had once been funding for community safety, that had since been syphoned somewhere else without it being accounted for. All I really needed was a small amount of money to cover mileage, expenses and the like.

The Chief was on my side and the rest were in a daze. Within a month I had a unit up and running with two sergeants, a constable and a civilian member of staff who had at one time been a police Chief Inspector. We were based in the headquarters of our Force Neighbourhood Watch Association.

I am sure that you will have heard of the Neighbourhood Watch. The stereotype is that of a collection of busy bodies who spy on their neighbours from behind twitching curtains. However, the reality, in our Force, was very different at that time. The Force Neighbourhood Watch had been created in the living room of a dynamic lady who also went on to become Chair of the Police Authority.

My unit and Neighbourhood Watch fitted together like hand and glove. We shared phones, computers, cups, kettles, paper and even a typist. It worked really well for three and a half years. Within a very short period of time my unit had details of all the partnerships that had been created across our Force area. We evaluated projects that were taking place and created a data base library of best practice. We also produced the first draft of a Force Children and Young People Strategy which was essential as corpocracy was crumbling into four separate, autonomous entities with very different working practices.

I was given a Chief Officer as my line commander and, though he was never highly impressed by what I did, he made himself accessible and provided a listening ear.

Then came 'Neighbourhood Policing,' fresh from the design rooms of Government with a requirement that all Forces would implement it within a year and a half. In some ways we were almost there with LPTs' but Neighbour Policing had all sorts of 'whistles, gongs and whiz bangs' that made it look more thought out and likely to succeed. I was sent to the early National meetings which were really aimed at Chief Officers. I became the Force fount of knowledge on this subject, and I quickly realized that we needed to project manage the implementation if we were to meet the required date.

Then as things were taking shape, the time came for the Chiefs' agreed departure, and it was to be all change and a new direction. Our new boss had attended the Special Course as I had. He had also served in the army and, though slight in stature, he fitted the type with a clipped moustache, resonant voice and short hair. I liked the man from the outset, he was no 'Limp Chief' or 'John Cleese' impersonator. Our new Chief was there to produce results after our Force had dream walked towards failure over the preceding years.

My first real meeting with the new guy was at a conference of all the Forces' management ranks and civilians. Divisional Commanders, Branch and Unit Managers all had the opportunity of addressing the assembled audience. I focused on Neighbourhood Policing so as to avoid being regarded as an 'ivory tower boffin' and my message was received with a round of applause.

The new Chief informed me, some years later, that he had been impressed by my message and style of presentation on that day. Unfortunately, from my career point of view, things continued to go downhill from that day. I will explore the reasons for my marginalization later, but the most obvious reason I was not flavour of the month was the pressure on the Chief to turn our performance round and restore our reputation as an achieving constabulary.

Our performance had declined as we struggled with LPTs' and the Home Secretary waged his war with our Chief of the time. New Labour had, as I have already stated, poured resources into the war on crime and disorder but they increasingly wanted to show their 'bang for the buck'. It seems to me that everyone and their dogs became involved in measuring police performance during the early 2000's.

There were a host of agencies, bodies and groups. There were the National Police Improvement Agency, Her Majesties' Inspectorate of Constabulary, the Audit Commission, the Policing Standards Unit and the Government Office to name just five. The NPIA was said to provide "a fundamental opportunity to reinvigorate and rationalise the relationship between Government, Forces and Police Authorities..." (Audit Commission.). The Government Office had been created by John Major in 1994 with the remit, among others, of being the primary means by which a range of police and disorder programmes are to be delivered in a region.

As the agencies set up to measure police performance proliferated so too did the number of measures that had to be applied. Police Forces were grouped into 'Families' with similar socio demographic footprints and these provided league tables by which Forces were judged. By any standard we looked pretty rubbish and things had got to get better. The Chief decided that all our resources would be thrown into making our performance improve. Everyone was sucked into the drive to make the Force perform, even I spent hours at the Forces' main performance meeting and a lot of good work was done there. However, I must say that the battle became bogged down in 'fiddling the figures' and dramatically altering the service that the Police once provided to the public.

The main players in the Force Performance Meeting were current and former senior detective officers. These were the figure fiddlers of old who had become persona non grata because of it. The closed CID shop that manipulated its' performance on paper had once become known as the 'Mafia' for its ability in shaping reality out of an illusion. We also had assistance from the NPIA who had a habit of recruiting officers to number crunching roles by promising them immediate or temporary promotion. Thus, we had inspectors, promoted to Chief Inspectors sent in to sort us out, when the implication was that our own Chief Officers and staff were incompetent.

One thing that the Chief Inspectors were good at was the picking out of 'star performing' Forces and then sending our Performance Team to look at the best practice that was operated there. The reality was that many of the old tricks, which had been eradicated because they had failed integrity tests, were brought back again. Innovative ways of deleting recorded crime, finding ways of 'detecting' when no one had any idea who had committed it and other such tricks again became the flavour of the day.

We came up with a thing called a 'sanctioned detection'. Those were crimes that could be detected by one approved means or another. Then there was a direction to officers that they should only deal with crimes that could be recorded as sanctioned detections. Huge swathes of crime were ignored, and some officers came to believe that the detection categories were the test of whether or not something even was a crime.

The fiddling worked and our Force began to rise up the league tables. I grumbled about the ethics of all this and I seemed to be a voice crying in the wilderness. As I write this in 2018 there has been an outcry about the Police Service under recording crime and incidents by upwards of ten percent. To that should be added another ten percent or more where people no longer bother to report their victimization because they believe, correctly, that the police will do nothing. This is where it started. At one meeting when I accused the team of deception the Chief said,

"Tell us we're wrong when you are sat on your beach in Cyprus!"

Well, I would say things were and are very wrong. I do understand the pressure placed on Forces by a Government desperate to be seen to be achieving and the Police Service always likes to be seen as a 'get it done' organization. For me the Government agencies should have seen all the mis practices removed so that all Forces were on a level playing field. Instead, we had the ethical copying the rogues and we were supposed to be the Police.

I am going to lighten things up a bit by sharing with you one or two real incidents that reflect what was happening in Policing. The first of these examples came as a personal slap to me. My wife and I had decided to replace the beech hedge at the bottom of our garden with a brick wall and a metal gate. The Chair of the Police Authority recommended a builder and he arrived promptly to give us a quote. A figure of two thousand five hundred pounds was agreed and I paid five hundred up fronts for the purchase of bricks and cement.

I took the hedge out and started to dig the footings while the builder arrived with a small quantity of bricks that he piled on my front lawn. Everything then stopped. I rang the builder over and over again without success until one day he turned up out of the blue with a few more bricks. He informed me that he had changed his phone, gave me a new number and he also told me that he had been having a few problems with his truck. The crux of all this was that he could not currently afford to have his vehicle repaired so he was working on jobs nearer his home. He suggested that if I could give him a bit more money 'up front' he could have the repairs done and get started on my wall straight away.

Now, all this did ring a few alarm bells but on balance he had been recommended by a very trustworthy source, he had returned to my house and given me his new contact details and I was desperate to have the wall up especially now that I had taken the hedge down. So, I gave him fifteen hundred pounds and went on holiday in the belief that the wall would be waiting when we returned.

You just know what I'm going to say don't you? I will not disappoint, there was no wall, no foundations and no extra delivery of bricks. He was not answering his phone again and eventually the number ceased to be recognized. I visited his provided address and, surprise, surprise, he had never lived there and was not known by the owner.

The front lawn was dead underneath the pile of bricks, the front garden looked like a wasteland covered in litter and it appeared that my two-thousand-pound investment was long gone. Now, the crime, which I still believe it to have been, was committed in the area in which I lived. I knew the inspector responsible for that area and he was a neighbour. However, I knew that the builder lived and worked from another area, so I phoned the inspector of that area. I was told that the facts would be reported as a crime and I would be updated when the builder was located.

I waited for two or three weeks, then I rang the station to which I had made the report and ended up totally shocked by what happened. I spoke to a sergeant, in the absence of the inspector, and was immediately informed that the facts I had reported did not constitute a crime and it would not be recorded as a crime. Further, he expressed the belief that if he shared any information that he had with me, then he would be liable to prosecution under the Data Protection Act. He stated his belief that I should just get on with my life. Now, you will remember (if you read my earlier book) that I trained as a lawyer and was at this time a Chief Superintendent. I had a pretty sound idea what constituted the offence of deception and had just suffered a fairly bad hit to the pocket. I told the sergeant that he was wrong and that even if the facts did not constitute the offence of deception, then the builder should still be interviewed.

I was then informed, by the sergeant I was talking to, that I was bullying him. This seemed unreal, all I wanted was the service that a normal member of the public would get. The sergeant was deciding off his own back that these facts were not a crime; an investigation, he felt, would result in him being the focus of a discipline and complaints case. I told him that he was wrong, and he then said he would be complaining about me.

That is exactly what happened, and I ended up in front of the Assistant Chief Constable. I said that the world had gone crazy. How could one fairly junior officer decide if something was a crime without even taking a statement from me. The 'criminal' was wandering about free, un interviewed, and I had no way of taking any other action.

This was my first hands on example of the state that the modern Police Service had come to. I was told that I could only have the same service as a member of the public. That was absolutely fine, but the members of the public were receiving a dire service. I was told I should take civil action against the builder, but I didn't know where he was and the sergeant, who I suspect knew, would not tell me because of Data Protection.

I took legal advice on this because I was too close to the facts to be impartial. The lawyer confirmed what I had thought. The facts revealed a strong suspicion of an offence having been committed, it should have been recorded, investigated and only 'No Crimed' after all the inquiries revealed an innocent state of mind on the part of the builder. I considered taking legal action against my Force, but I backed away and employed a new builder who did the job just as he said he would.

So, you may think what you like. I felt that I was a victim of crime. My Force never recorded it so their figures lacked one crime from their total that year. You may also guess just how many other 'crimes' were also ignored, never recorded or forgotten about. In my opinion officers were ignoring the law and taking Force operating procedures as the decisive 'bible' on what would and would not get dealt with. The Police had become legislators and that was never meant to happen.

I will leave the personal hurt of that incident and move onto another which may make the case even better. There are certainly numerous upset and disappointed victims out there.

An Irishman left the Republic of Ireland and travelled to the UK. There he hired a flat backed lorry. He purchased a top of the range, but second hand, hot tub and placed it on the back of the truck. He then acquired a lot of leaflets advertising a particular brand of hot tubs and, whilst collecting those, he obtained from somewhere a set of plans approved by a council for siting such a tub.

The Irishman was now a fully-fledged entrepreneur and he hit the streets to sell as many tubs as possible. He promised that the products he used were a market leader, he offered them at half the market price, and he fitted them for free. He also promised to provide full plans prior to delivery and fitting of the tubs.

In Nottingham several people agreed to purchase a tub and handed over two thousand pounds. They were provided a set of plans and an official looking receipt for the money. Sadly, they never received a tub and they never saw the Irishman again. The victims all trotted off to the Police but by this time our entrepreneur was in another Force area on his grand tour of the north of England.

Our area was visited and soon after his arrival several people each handed over two thousand pounds. One of the victims made himself known to me and he informed me that the Police would not be taking any action. He had been told that he was not a victim of crime. I made enquiries and got several versions of why no action would be taken. Firstly, the facts were said not to constitute a crime and that was even more amazing than my case. Secondly, I was told that, as fraud was not a priority crime, the Force would spend no resources on it. Finally, I reached someone who had been involved in making the Force policy. He said that unless the fraud involved a sum over twenty thousand pounds and both the victim, and the offender lived in our area there would be no action.

So, some officers believed that they did not need to crime a report because it was not priority crime. Some believed that they did not need to 'crime it' because there was no chance of a 'sanctioned detection'. Most significantly, as the offender was not a British national, he could commit offences in any Force with the same policy that we had, and he would never be investigated. Further as each victim in this case only paid up two thousand pounds the offender would have been home free even if he had been British.

I am certain that much will have been done to put things right in ensuring that crimes are properly reported and investigated but, as I have already said, thousands of victimisations that should have been 'crimed' have slipped through the net.

Finally, and just to update what I have been saying. A little over a year ago my wife's car was parked, on the road, outside our house, overnight. When we went out something did not look right with the car. When I felt a scratch on the bumper a large section of the chrome stripping fell off. The rear windscreen wiper was also laying on the road, the roof was dented, the windscreen was cracked, and we could see footmarks on the back of the car. We assumed that someone had run over the car, which is a regular pastime in our area these days. The damage would cost well in excess of a thousand pounds to put right, so we went to the police station to report the crime.

I gave all the details, and an 'Occurrence Sheet' was raised on the computer. I was told that a Police Community Support Officer or a Police Officer would call and see me. One of those officers would give me a crime number for our insurance. A year later we are still waiting for the visit and the damage was never 'crimed.' Strangely, in this case the Police got things right even without speaking to us. For as we returned home from the Police Station a neighbour came out and told me he had filmed the aftermath of the damage on his mobile phone.

We were shown a man picking up a cycle from the road at the back of my wife's car. He was obviously the worse for drink and it looked like he had cycled into the back of the car and been thrown over the roof and onto the windscreen and bonnet. The cyclist tried to put the damaged bits back into the car before cycling off into the night.

So there really was no crime on this occasion, it should have been a road traffic accident and that was never reported either. In theory there should still be an Occurrence Sheet waiting for a clearance, but then I am certain it will have slipped through after a year.

Whilst reviewing the text of this book prior to publication I was made aware of a very recent incident. This represents another aspect of figure fiddling in the extreme.

A gentleman went to see a retired officer to explain what had happened to him. He was told that he was the victim of a theft, and he should report it at the nearest police station. A day later the gentleman attended at the nearest police station to his home and that station also happened to be Police Headquarters. After a short wait he was seen and allowed to recount what had happened. The officer firstly tried to inform the gentleman that he was not a victim of crime, then he changed tack. The officer informed the gentleman that he would have to go home and report the 'crime' online. So, it seems that at some stations it is impossible for the police to record crime!

The gentleman went home, recorded the crime online and two hours later he received an e mail message saying that the crime had been filed because of the lack of evidence.

Clearly, if the Police do not recognise crime as such and do not record it when it is reported and do not investigate it when it is recorded, what is going on?

So, dear Chief, I told you so all those years ago. It was really figure fiddling that improved the Forces' performance and we let the public down badly, didn't we? I wrote that sentence on a beach in Cyprus, (or at least very near one.).

CHAPTER EIGHTEEN

INTRIGUE IN HIGH PLACES

If you have had enough about performance, then switch off for a minute. I seemed to be a negative voice crying in the wilderness every time that performance was mentioned, yet what did the Force do? They sent me to a meeting, held once a week in Leeds at Government Office. To discuss, yes, you've guessed, performance.

All the Yorkshire Police Forces, apart from ours, sent a Chief Officer to these meetings so I was sent as a sort of champion to hold our head up! I can only guess that someone thought of Government Office as a partnership agency and not a real performance driver. Most of my Chief Officers saw Partnership as 'pink and fluffy stuff', not real policing.

Government Office was there to see that central Government initiatives were driven through, crime and disorder were just one of the many themes they pursued, but that was the full extent of my involvement with them. They were headed by someone titled as the 'Crime Tsar' and shortly after I started attending the meetings a female took over that post. She had no previous experience in policing and had worked on the Government response to the Foot and Mouth crisis. Most of the people who worked there seemed to know nothing about policing, with the majority of the staff being drafted in from the NHS or central Government.

It would be easy to ridicule Government Office for their lack of hand on knowledge, but they did bring a fresh approach. They were good people who wanted to make a difference, they listened to what you said and most importantly they had pots of money to help out with initiatives. I ended up with someone from Government Office working in my offices to produce a Partnership Drug Strategy and he really knew what he was doing, but I will come back to him shortly.

Eventually Chief Officers woke up to the fact that Government Office had a fair degree of clout, and I was sent back to my box to get on with Neighbourhood Policing and 'community things'. My team were producing everything I had asked them to. We produced a monthly update on the progress of partnership across the Force, we had produced several draft strategies, we had a delivery schedule for Neighbourhood Policing, we supported the development of Neighbourhood Watch, and we developed a problem-solving course for those who were to be Neighbourhood Officers.

From my point of view community safety was a growth area. Since the Crime and Disorder Act there had been a huge upsurge in the numbers of those working in community safety related jobs. There was, however, no guidance to would be employees or employers about the skills that the new workers would require. At this time an organisation was set up to provide support and guidance to those working in community safety across the country. That body was the Community Safety Network.

The CSN was largely voluntary, but it did have a core staff who were paid, and it was led by a Chief Executive. I was impressed by all those who worked with the CSN and after a year working with them, I became a director of the organization. I had permission from my Chief Officer to get involved and I suppose the Force must have gained some kudos. I was also a member of the Rural Communities Forum, which worked to ensure rural areas were not sold short when receiving their slice of resources. I loved working on these non-police bodies, and I also went on to join the committee of the National Neighbourhood Watch Association.

While my job just seemed to get bigger the work of my unit focused more and more on Neighbourhood Policing. This was more than creating a few local bases as LPT's had become. It involved a total acceptance of partnership working, joint problem solving, a real involvement of members of the local communities and the total focus being on making a difference.

As I typed the preceding paragraph, I thought to myself that I was writing the sort of buzz words and bullshit that I had been spoon fed as a police officer. However, these words meant real things if everyone joined in and made it work. Our last Chief had created a network of local police bases funded by the Police Authority, so we needed to get social workers, refuse workers, wardens, school caretakers all involved in solving particular problems. We had to share all our information, help people with their problems and ask them for their help with ours.

I had a thorough grasp of what was needed, my staff had bought into what needed to be done and all our other work spun out of Neighbourhood Policing. So, for example, we were working with Neighbourhood Watch to recruit and train a body of volunteers who would work in the new police bases to increase opening hours and enable officers to spend more time on the streets. This was the symbiosis I mentioned earlier, we helped Neighbourhood Watch design the course and they provided them and were paid by the Police. The more recruits Neighbourhood Watch recruited the more courses they had to run and the more money they earned for other projects. We opened police stations that had been closed for years and the basic administrative duties were performed by the volunteers.

Similarly, it was around this time that Police Community Support Officers started to be discussed as a concept that might take off. The idea was that the service provided by fully trained police officers should be supplemented with a body of people who would have some of the police powers but definitely with no power of arrest.

The idea evolved because police officers seldom got out of their cars, the public rarely saw a uniform police presence walking the street and almost no one was able to report that they had spoken to a police officer in years. PCSO's were to reintroduce a uniform presence that could be seen, talked to and have more time to solve the real problems encountered at community level.

I cannot claim that the project in my Force was driven by me. There was an absolutely first-class inspector who had worked in training, and he was totally committed to PCSO's. He did come and talk to me when he had ideas and hopefully, I was able to open a few doors and gain support for him. Together we agreed that the practical side of training PCSO'S should be delivered in a real location and a shopping mall that fitted the bill was located. The public must have been a little perturbed by what was going on; there were drunken disputes, fly tipping, shoplifting, missing people, fighting, traffic collisions and a host of other incidents. Fortunately, there were dozens of police officers and innumerable PCSO's and the training went well.

PCSO's were a sitting target for the many critics that the idea attracted. A Tory MP came and witnessed our training programme in action. He grumbled and mumbled, looked surly and was generally obnoxious. He was interviewed by the local newspaper and ripped into PCSO's as if they were a dark and alien force who were being introduced to dilute Policing and undermine the ages old Constitution of the United Kingdom. He secured allies in the Police Federation who saw PCSO's as a threat to the role of constable.

I guess the Tories had to oppose PCSO's as it was not their idea but gradually the concept caught hold. Some Councils and Shopping Centres paid for their own PCSO's. Ours were a wonderful bunch of people and many of them went on to become fully fledged Police Officers within a year or so. They formed the basis of the new Neighbourhood Policing Teams, and I am not certain where we would be today without them.

All these things and more were going on within my Unit and there was a constant buzz of activity. We struggled to get Chief Officer support for the strategies we designed (even though they were adopted by some other Forces and pedalled by Government Office as 'best practice') but in general terms we were up with the game and delivering to schedule.

Then one day, as I arrived at the offices, I noticed a change in the atmosphere as I came through the door. No one spoke to me and as I entered my office and I quickly discovered what was different. A Chief Inspector sat at my desk, all my papers, photographs, teacup and uniform were heaped in cardboard boxes at one end of the room. I was momentarily speechless and then I exploded.

It transpired that the Chief Inspector had just arrived back in Force from a secondment overseas and the 'Chinless Wonder' had told him to take over the 'roll out' of Neighbourhood Policing. Unfortunately, no one had bothered to tell me that he was coming. It was clear that he had been assured I would be out of the office before he arrived.

Neighbourhood Policing was my pet. It was woven through everything that my Unit did, take it away and the rest would fall down as a collection of bits.

I know that no one is indispensable, and I am well aware of the old adage about putting your hand in a bucket of water and taking it out again, everything is as it was. However, everything in those offices were my creations. I rang my Chief Officer, and he knew what had been planned. They were trying to find me an office in another building. I asked if I had done anything wrong and he said that was not the case and he was delighted by what had been achieved.

For three days I worked from home. No one rang me or came to see me. It was suddenly as if I had developed the plague. Then I was told that my new office was ready, and I drove over with the box full of my uniform and papers in the boot of my car.

I arrived at a rambling Victorian building overlooking a large park. It had been acquired as a base for one of the Local Policing Teams that had been introduced so suddenly. A lot of money had been spent bringing that building into the twenty first century, but I am not sure it was fulfilling any purpose when I went there. A sergeant was waiting for me when I arrived and he presented me with a key to the office I had been allocated, he then left, and I never spoke to anyone else in that building all the time I had the office at my disposal. It was not that I was antisocial or that anyone dodged me, there was no one there. The public must have been totally bemused by the presence of this large police building in their midst, perhaps even they knew better than to request any assistance from there.

I did a lot of reading, I caught up with the annual assessment reports of the few staff who still answered to me, and I completed two strategies that no one ever read. I attended the opening and closing of PCSO courses, went to all the major Force meetings and no one bothered me. I arrived at the office at 0900 hours, and I left at 1700 hours, it was the most turgid routine I had ever adhered to, and it was totally dispiriting.

Then one day, about a month after I arrived in my new office, I was visited by two of my staff from the Neighbourhood Watch offices. They said that they had come to see how I was. I made them a coffee and we chatted away in an informal and sociable way until one of them asked me where the Chief Inspector was?

I had no idea. I had been told not to interfere with his role and I had not even visited the offices I used to occupy. I had assumed he would be there working away on the plan that I had left behind. I had felt that I had been abandoned but what they now told me portrayed a very different picture. My staff felt that they had no job, and they were worried that someone would eventually turn up and ask them what they had been doing. Indeed, a request had been received from the Home Office for an update on the progress of Neighbourhood Policing, it still sat on the Chief Inspectors' desk, and it was now overdue.

It was upsetting to have my visitors so clearly upset and bewildered by what was going on. However, I felt as if they had now transferred a great weight to me. I was still their 'Boss' but I had been told not to get involved with the project they were working on. If I rang a Chief Officer, then it would look like I had disobeyed my instructions and it would certainly look like I was pulling the rug out from under the feet of the Chief Inspector.

I told them I would have a think about what could be done, and I gave them some tasks to get on with until I got back to them. I then sat and did exactly what I said I would do. I thought and thought about it with no solution leaping into my mind, until out of the blue the phone rang. I had almost forgotten I had a phone in my new office, as it had rung so infrequently during my period of exile. This call was an important one. It was from a police officer attached to the national team for monitoring and assisting the roll out of the Neighbourhood Policing Project. We shared a common friend and had met at several previous conferences.

I was asked what was happening in our Force as he had not received a response to his request for an update. He had tried to ring me in my old offices but had never had his calls answered.

I told him exactly what the position was, and he could not believe that I was no longer in charge. It was a long conversation, but the outcome was that either he or his manager would ring my Force Headquarters and ask Chief Officers what was happening.

Two days later I was called to see my Chief Officer and I was informed that I was to retake control of the Neighbourhood Policing Project. The Chief Inspector had moved on, there was no suggestion that he had failed to deliver nor was there any mention of national interest in our lack of progress. The reality was that he had moved to a CID post which is where he had always wanted to be, and he had never had any interest in the job he had been given. The blame lay with the person who decided to interfere with a team that was working. Was the decision made in the best interests of the Force or out pure malice and spite? Only they can answer that question.

One thing was certain was that there was a lot of catching up to be done. The Force had been bogged down with performance issues, so now we were all hands to the pump with Neighbourhood Policing. I now had to arrange a conference at which the Force would launch its' Neighbourhood Policing programme. I booked a college premises with a large hall and over two hundred officers were to attend. County Hall, the Police Improvement Agency and two MPs were to attend. The Chief was to speak, as was I and on the day the itinerary ran like clockwork. Police officers always like to be well fed at training days and even that was a great success.

On conclusion of the day my back was sore with the patting and my head could have exploded with the compliments that came my way. There was a real buzz about the audience after the conference ended and it felt as if we were on the edge of achieving something really good. There was, however, a lot to be done in driving things forward across the Force area, creating training documents, operating guidance and the like.

I also noted that another superintendent had arrived in my teams' offices. He had been sent by the Chief to produce a national drugs strategy. In one sense this was a stand-alone piece of work. The Chief was the head of the Drugs Business Area in ACPO (Association of Chief Police Officers) and it fell to him to create the guidance that all Forces would follow. However, I already had someone from Government Office working on a strategy for partnerships tackling drugs issues. There clearly would be a lot of overlap and the two could have worked together very closely.

The fact that the Police Drug Strategy was written in splendid isolation from developments in other areas summed up the way my Chief Officers worked. The superintendent and the man from the Government Office sat in the same office and to the best of my knowledge never spoke to each other. I tried to bring the two strands together and one side was willing, but the police side wanted to write the strategy and explain it afterwards. I think with the police there is often the question of ownership and taking credit becoming mixed in with career progression. Sometimes, in a dream I have, a police officer reports on a paper he has written and then as the audience applaud his face distorts and he becomes a demented, raving monster crying out, "its' mine, all mine!"

Anyway, let's move on. My time in the 'isolation box' office had given me time to think about partnership working. It became clear to me that if all the agencies involved in the Crime and Disorder Partnerships (CDRP'S) were to use the problem-solving model then all of us needed a better means of sharing information.

The police downloaded crime information onto discs once a month and circulated those to the four unitary authorities (Councils) which covered our Force area. The information was sanitized with all personal identification factors removed. We received nothing from our partners unless we specifically asked.

It struck me that the CDRP's would function better if they had their own computer system with all the partnership information downloaded onto it. The problems that had been identified by the public could also be logged onto the computer and a record kept of all actions taken to resolve them. Such a computer would have completed the joining up of the parts of the CDRPs' in a meaningful way.

I drafted a quick report to my Chief Officers, spoke to the Chairs of the CDRPs' and had a meeting with the Force IT people. Everyone seemed to like the idea and it was worth doing some more work on the idea. A project of this nature would really attract some positive attention from those who had been condemning our performance. Government Office in Leeds were particularly supportive, and all the doors appeared to be opening.

The idea started like a snowball at the top of a mountain, and it got bigger and bigger as it rolled down the slope. Within days I was asked what the cost would be, and I had no idea whatsoever. We were talking about developing something across four councils, the police and several other 'players'. There was no single person who had a grasp of all the different systems that were run across that group of people.

I did believe that the councils would contribute financially but the 'seed' money would have to come from us. I expected a Project Group to be set up to research, plan and stage the introduction of the idea. However, madness season was about to close in on us. There was already an impetus growing to deliver the new system and I was called back to Chief Officers meeting. There was only one question that interested anyone. "In broad brushstrokes, how much would the Police have to put up to get things moving?"

I should have stuck to my earlier position, that I had no idea whatsoever. However, the pressure to come up with what one Chief Officer called a 'guesstimation' was incredible. I had already introduced the Force Crime Pattern Analysis system and that had cost a million pounds. I assumed that this new idea would be similar and so there was the figure that I plucked out of the air.

Everyone knew how much of a guess that figure had been and further everyone knew that the Force did not have signed agreements from the councils to participate. All we had was a vague idea, a good level of support in principle and absolutely nothing concrete to fall back onto.

The Chief Officers schedule required that they placed a paper before the next police Authority Meeting. If not, they had no chance of being allocated money for the new system in the next financial year. I do not know who wrote the paper and I do not know what it said. I just got on with chatting to the key players across the councils so that interest levels would no fall away. Then, to my amazement I was told that the million pounds had been approved and the project was up and running.

At that juncture, exit stage left, all the Chief Officers were too busy to be involved. It felt like I was standing at the end of a plank on a pirate ship. The rest is chaos! I managed to pull a meeting together with representatives from all those who would benefit from the proposed system. However, those present were a mixed bunch. Some were computer technicians, some were social workers, one was the head of a CDRP, one was the Chief Executive of a council. Most of those present did not have the authority to sign even an agreement in principle. The majority had no idea how it could be done.

I asked my IT Department to come up with what information they would require from all four councils. In turn the IT Department asked me for a 'specification' for the system. I told them what I wanted it to do, but that was not a specification, they wanted details, operating systems etc.... I asked if they could help with the specification but apparently, they did not write them they simply delivered them. Chief Officers seemed not to understand the problem, and, in any event, they were still busy 'off stage.'

I approached the CDRP in the Division I knew best and bit by bit a specification emerged with a fairly realistic cost attached to it. Then, thinking the problem was cracked, I visited Chief Executives, or their representatives and this is where the attempt to weave air began.

Neighbouring councils are rivals; indeed, many councils see their peers as the enemy. They talk of each other in 'scented words' but agreement between them is all but impossible. All the councils liked the idea, all of them wanted some of the police 'pot of gold' but all of them wanted to sign up to a specification that they themselves had developed. Any sort of agreement looked light years away.

By this time my Chief Officers were touring the country with another stage group and were completely unavailable. So, I asked the CDRP who had produced a specification to run it as a pilot and see if reality could emerge from the plan. They would play! Great joy! I had nudged us twenty five percent of the way to the finishing line. Sadly, that is as far as I ever got. A year after the money was allocated next to nothing had been spent. Each council was ferreting away on its' own with the pilot surging ahead of the rest.

All four councils provided a system to their CDRPs' though it took many months for them to be in place. I was retired before they were all up and working and they looked very different from each other. I guess I had failed to deliver but how many ideas turn out exactly as they were first envisioned. If I had not tried to kick start the introduction of an information system that would support problem solving, then it could have taken years not months for one to arrive.

The Chief Officers never said to me that I had failed or let them down. I do know that they would have to explain to the Police Authority why a chunk of money was not spent and as a group they never liked criticism being applied to them.

Four months after the removal of the Chief Inspector I turned up at work one day to find a superintendent sat at my desk. He had been promoted to take over management of the Neighbourhood Policing Project, the Chief Officers had done it again. This time the Chinless Wonder was definitely the authority behind the change in command. He had come out from hiding and shown his hand.

I was left with one sergeant and no real job. I became a sort of Force Representative. I attended conferences, meetings I knew nothing about, Church Services, dinners with people I did not know. Very quickly I felt like I had already retired and one day a constable asked me if I had.

I was again told that I was not to be involved with Neighbourhood Policing, indeed the team were moved to a former LPT base on the very edge of the Force area. I had created a series of 'stakeholder meetings'; these were members of the public taken from a cross section of a particular community and their purpose was to operate as a sounding board to test the aims and objectives of Neighbourhood Policing against. After I was removed from post the meetings never took place again, the Force delivered what it wanted not what the public said they wanted.

Then out of the blue I snapped. I asked for an appointment to see the Chief Constable, was allocated a slot and arranged to be accompanied by a colleague from the Superintendents' Association. I wanted to know what had been going on and why it had gone on for so long without anyone telling me what I had done.

The Chief did not dodge any of my questions and I must say I always regarded him as one of the good guys from the moment of his arrival. Surprisingly, he sang my praises too. He had liked my presentation at the first conference he had pulled together in Force. He had looked forward to working with me and was saddened that it had taken so long trying to put the Forces' performance back on track. Further, he had arranged a great career opportunity for me. I could, if I wished, be seconded to Government Office. There I could work on the development of Neighbourhood Policing and partnership working across all the Forces in the Yorkshire and the Humber region.

This was exactly what I would have wanted. By pushing initiatives through at County level, I would effectively have greater control over what would be happening in my own Force. I would also be out of the way of the Chinless Wonder who the Chief intimated was less than enamoured with me. So, having been offered my dream job, I sat there for a couple of minutes and then handed my resignation in!

Why did I do that? A year later I wished I hadn't, and it would have been a whole new challenge. At that point in time my confidence was at a low ebb. I had effectively been removed from a job I loved and in which I thought I was a success. If the Force didn't want me, then I didn't want them. I interpreted the Chiefs' offer as a way of getting me out of the Force. I would be travelling long distances every day of the week and I had hated that as Divisional Commander. I also didn't want my friends and colleagues to forget about me; I had remained in one Force for thirty years and I wanted to leave while I still felt part of it. Looking back, I made a massive mistake which I can add to the many career mistakes I have accumulated along the way.

Strangely, I was instructed to attend a First Aid course on my last five working days in the Police. A complete waste of money for the Force but I enjoyed it. It was great mixing with a cross section of the Force in a relaxed environment. I heard the opinions of those there on a number of subjects, but I recall their views on the Chinless Wonder with a smile. I discovered that his nickname with most of this group was the 'Pilsbury Doughboy' (an advertising mascot from the Pilsbury Company appearing in many commercials from 1965 to 2005. It was a rotund white figure and the adverts concluded with a human finger poking the Doughboys stomach as he dissolves in an explosion of giggling) and that just about sums him up.

Three months after my meeting with the Chief I handed my warrant card, key to the Forces' police buildings, uniform and other equipment over to an employee in the Force stores. I then walked out, no longer a police officer.

CHAPTER NINETEEN

OUTSIDE

The big question that I have never been able to fully answer is whether or not I miss being a police officer?

I missed it physically the first day after I had left the Force. Getting up in the morning seemed to lack a sense of urgency or purpose. I had lots to do but nothing that really needed to be done. I felt as if I was in the way at home, under my wife's feet, an unproductive unit!

That feeling will probably have been shared by anyone who has worked hard in any job and then just stopped. I do, however, feel that leaving the police is somehow more final than leaving the majority of jobs. For example, if you are a plumber, or an electrician or a decorator you can 'do a bit' to keep your hand in. As former police officer you cannot just pop out and do a bit of thief taking to make you feel alive.

When you join the Police Service it is a little like joining a secret society. Most people have never been inside a police station and only gain an insight through documentaries or TV drama. When you join you are sworn on oath to serve the Queen, you are allowed to exercise exclusive powers, you are given a card that shows that you belong and a key that lets you into almost every building in the Force. On the first day that you arrive at your station, passing those waiting for service, you let yourself in. You identify yourself by that very act. I am sure that in their first days, every officer feels six feet tall as they walk through the public and enter the secret side of the station.

The uniform sets you aside from the public and makes you a bit special. Members of the public expect you to be endowed with almost superhuman powers that can be used to solve their problems. As a police officer you may share that opinion, once you have survived the first incident you went to.

You quickly learn a new language which sets you aside from the public. When you enter a police station on arriving at work you acquire a status, you are 10 and 1 (on duty at the police station). This was part of the Ten Code which required learning by heart, if you were contacted and told to 10 and 3 you were required to contact your station: 10 and 2, you had to physically go to the station.

An interesting code was 10 and 7, this denoted that the receiver of a radio message found it unintelligible. However, usage gave it another meaning. If an officer is dealing with someone who is either slow, has mental issues or learning needs then he will tell the station that he is dealing with someone who is 10 and 7 with heavy interference. Totally unacceptable these days.

Another set of codes referred to the nature of the incident that was being described, so a Code 4 was a burglary, a Code 2 was a robbery. There were codes for almost everything including a Code 19 which was to tell the sergeant that a cup of tea was waiting for them in the station.

I should point out that the Codes I have referred to so far were specific to my Force. There is an ACPO Ten Code that is rather different to the one we used to use. However, all Forces use the phonetic alphabet, Alpha, Beta, Charlie, Delta, Echo etc.

An officer who is out on patrol can go several hours without being seen by another police officer. In the days before radio officers walked round their beat in a set order and were supposed to be at set points at prescribed times. They would often be met by a sergeant at one of the points and their ONB (Officers Notebook) would be checked and signed. Even nowadays sergeants will radio officers and ask them to meet them for a "point". The signing of the notebook is called a "chalk".

Some of the secret language can still cause a smile. A constable could be asked, "Do you want a gobble?" The reply might me "Is there a day off in lieu?" A gobble referred to working overtime. There was a book known as the "Gobble Book," in which officers would put their names down next to shifts where they were willing to work on their rest days (days off). If you worked a Bank Holiday, you got a day's pay and a day off in lieu.

On arriving at work for a 'briefing,' officers were required to 'show their appointments' (handcuffs, truncheon and notebook).

Further officers, like the military, use acronyms. ETA means expected time of arrival, RTA was a road traffic accident although there are now no such things as all crashes are collisions.... they are never an accident. NFA would be no further action and often an irritated officer would record a 'job' they had been allocated as NFI ('No F----r in'.)

The further you go into a police station the further you are from the public and the more secret your world becomes. The Charge Office with its own rituals, the interview rooms, the CID rooms with their laughter and thick layer of blue smoke. Everyone and everywhere in a police station has a part to play in the drama that goes on there and you quickly learn what is expected of you by your colleagues.

In public there are people who will need you and they depend on you doing the right thing or setting the correct machinery in motion. The organization expects that you perform your duties in a correct way and your colleagues depend on you to do so. The higher through the ranks you go, so you owe a bigger duty to those who work for you; they depend on you just as you depend on them to achieve a desired outcome. You all belong to the organization, and it will be there when you have gone but it feels like you will always be there and part of it forever.... until that day when suddenly you aren't anymore.

After the physical wrench of not being part of it anymore, you are left with time to think. No longer do you dwell on whether or not you miss being a police officer, you start to wonder about Policing itself. What is it for? Does it achieve its' objectives? Does it meet the needs of those who depend on it?

For me the Police Service is like someone wandering, alone and lost in a thick, impenetrable mist. It has become bemused, bothered and bewildered by an environment that has become much more complex than it was ever designed to deal with.

There appears to be no way back to the halcyon days of Policing because the world of those days has also gone. I still care what happens to it and to that extent I miss being a police officer, but I do not like what it has become.

For what it is worth I will share my views on what Policing has become or what has become of it. Perhaps what I will say will be seen as a lament for a lost age, but I am not deluded enough to know that we ever got it right in the past. Now, however, the lunatics seem to be free in the asylum and they have no idea where they are going.

CHAPTER TWENTY

I have never liked Tony Blair. I do not like a waiter/waitress in a restaurant telling me to "have a nice day" or the NHS telling me to "eat your greens, they're good for you". I just do not like artificial things that do not belong in the real world.

When I first listened to Blair, I was entranced. He seemed fresh, full of energy, willing to listen and keen to make a difference. However, that buzz lasted all of fifteen minutes. Then I started to realise that I was being sold froth. Everything was a sales pitch, platitudes, sound bites and absolutely no substance or plan to move forward with.

After several years of his government, I was totally disenchanted and could not even listen to him anymore and my antipathy towards him could have got me into trouble. I went to a conference at the Queen Elizabeth Conference Centre, in London, which was supposed to be an update on Neighbourhood Policing. There were a number of prominent speakers, but right from the start we were treat like children. We were informed that if we behaved and were very lucky, we would have a surprise.

I just knew that that surprise would be one of Blair's flying visits to gain some positive media coverage and bombard an audience with delusional spume. I told a colleague that if he arrived, I would leave. I was certain that he would not miss me. Every half an hour or so we were reminded that we were still being good, and the treat was getting nearer. Then half an hour before proceedings were due to be concluded we were let into the surprise. Yes, you've got it. Tony was on his way.

I put my papers in my briefcase and set off out of the lecture room. As I entered the auditorium a number of people closed in on me. They informed me that I would miss the Prime Minister if I left, and they were not impressed when I said I was not that bothered. I was told to leave quickly, if I had to, and obviously I did not move quickly enough. Tony Blair and I passed each other in the doorway going in opposite directions. There were glares from his aides and security staff before I found myself enclosed by a crowd of cheering public, clicking cameras and the whole media circus.

My wife had been watching the news and had seen me on Sky News, so, unfortunately, had the Chief. My early departure was noted with amusement rather than annoyance, so I had had two lucky escapes in one afternoon! However, it was on the train journey home from my brush with 'Power' that I started to think about what had gone wrong with the Police Service.

In the early years of the reign of Queen Victoria the Police Service was slowly evolving. The streets of London were far from safe and those with anything worth stealing would only venture out if they or their servants were armed. Yet in spite of the flourishing criminal classes there was widespread resistance to the introduction of the Police.

That word, Police, brought to the mind of the British population the secret Force that had been operated in France during the chaotic years after the French Revolution. There a network of operatives spied on the public, denounced people who held views that did not fit with their paymasters and carried out their arrests in the middle of the night. Britain wanted nothing to do with such an alien growth operating within our shores.

The Police Force that evolved in Britain placed great emphasis on its' officers being seen as citizens in uniform with limited powers and the focus being on prevention and protection. The uniform that evolved was based on the everyday dress of ordinary men about their business. A formal suit with a top hat and only an arm band to designate the fact that the officer was on duty.

In spite of this low-key introduction there were still widespread anti police riots. A police officer who tried to prevent a bare-knuckle boxing match taking place was killed. No one was punished as the court decided that the police officer was exceeding his powers by interfering with a lawful assembly.

A little under two hundred years later the Police are once again the butt of criticism, with their popularity ratings falling by the day. However, in the period between the introduction of the Police and the present day they became widely regarded as the best Police Service in the world; strong on impartiality, integrity and freedom from political interference.

So, what went wrong? Did society end up with the Police Service it deserved? Did leadership standards fall? Did governments fail to provide a clear steer as to what was expected? Did the Police Service just lose its' way in a changing environment where no one understood what was meant by consensus anymore? Could it be an amalgam of all these factors?

In the 1950's Britain was recovering from a horrendous war. There was little wealth to go round, rationing was still in place, but the Welfare State was underway with the National Health Service being the flagship of a brave new world. For the Police, crime levels were low, and the emphasis was on helping people and resolving problems rather than invoking the letter of the law.

Then the 1960's changed everything; a culture of youth took over and to the driving back beat of rock and roll, consumerism hit society in a big way. Fashionable clothes, drink, drugs, more available vehicles and leisure activities were all required in large quantities. To the young the Police became the 'Fuzz', the 'Plod', the 'Pigs' and the 'them and us scenario' had arrived and was there to stay.

Obviously, to try and encapsulate dramatic social change in a few paragraphs is grossly oversimplifying the reality but the effort is worthwhile because it provides a broad brush back drop to the present.

In 1964 the Royal Commission on Policing issued its' report and set the model for the then modern Police Service. To a large extent it is still the model now. In spite of enormous social and political change new policing initiatives have been 'bolt ons' and that is where the main error lies. I have heard government after government bang on about reforming the police, but their efforts have been piecemeal, patch and mend, stretching the same money even further and diluting everything while never asking 'Joe Public" what they really wanted.

Tony Blair's Governments sum up the failure of our national leaders to provide the direction that is required. Blair really wanted things to get better but like all politicians he was in a hurry. Real change is a slow process, but Governments are elected for five years and if the public are not happy then the next election could well see another government.

Blair swept to power on a lot of sound bites, such as "Save the NHS", but behind the jargon there was little about how it would be done. Money was undoubtedly spent, particularly on the NHS, but waiting lists continued to grow, people died of diseases caught in hospitals and more died through neglect. The money appeared to be going into a black hole for all that was being achieved. The Cabinet was not allowed to discuss the NHS, and, in the end, I think Blair lost interest and moved on; being a diplomat seemed easier and ultimately more profitable than being a national leader.

What was needed at the outset was a plan for the future of the NHS. A long-term plan, with objectives and a staged implementation. If there was one, I never heard of it and I am not certain we are any clearer at this day. It is also possible to confuse this picture by accusing politicians of being liars and Blair's inner circle were excellent at that. I remember some twenty billion pounds being promised to the NHS and everyone thought the problem would be solved. The money had arrived by magic from the wand of Gordon Brown. There was, in reality, no twenty billion pounds. There was a figure of around eight billion pounds in year one and it went on the same things in the second year and the third year, then in the fourth year who knows?

Crime and Disorder should have been simpler and from the partnership side of things there were enormous successes. However, so much of the money was only for one or two years, so what happened then? The stretched budget of a council or Police Force cannot recruit new staff for a five-year plan if they are only given new funding for two years. The result was that many schemes started and never finished and in some cases pots of money were returned because borrowing against an unknown tomorrow was robbing Peter to pay Paul.

Many initiatives in Crime and Disorder were the sort of bolt ons that I have already referred to. Everyday policing still had to go on, so if the new initiative has to be carried out then something else must stop. To ensure delivery was taking place the Blair regime placed even greater emphasis on performance indicators.

I have already provided my views on performance indicators and the way in which they distort the service that is delivered and has led to police officers ignoring whole swathes of crime. The excessive reliance placed on performance indicators can be a little sinister in other ways as careers have depended on what the figures say.

In 2006 my Force was the worst performing area in England and Wales. The Performance Teams' meetings and visits round the country resulted in a twenty percent reduction in crime by 2009. The Force had made it back into the top eight areas in the country! What wonders had been achieved! If the public do not report crime or incidents, then that is good news; if the Police can find a way of not recording an incident that is reported then so much the better (remember my wall?) and if you only record that which can be detected then you are in heaven!

I have already suggested that detectives have had a long history of 'fiddling' figures. My Chief Inspector, from the toilets, became a leader in the massaging of the Forces' performance management. He had once belonged to a group known as the 'Mafia' who were renowned for manipulating crime statistics. On his retirement he was given a role as the head of the Force Criminal Justice Unit (a civilian post.) His efforts in improving performance had clearly been greatly valued and it must be said that he was also an excellent detective.

Now you may recall that certain indiscretions resulted in the imprisonment of this individual. In court at his trial one witness said that there was a fear of giving evidence against him because of the existence of a CID Mafia that still influenced the Force. There was also a strong suggestion that some of the Forces' Chief Officers believed that it would have been against the public interest for the accused ex Chief Superintendent to appear in court. The fear was that he could throw "lots of mud" at the Force.

What would that mud have been? Could it be that some of the Chief Officers had behaved in a way similar to that of the accused? Did the Chief Officers encourage an atmosphere in which behaviour of that sort would be tolerated? Had one or more of the Chief Officers done something even more heinous than the accused? Or could it just relate to the organisation's distortion of the official statistics?

By 2015 the Force was back in the mire from a performance perspective. The HMI reported that "officer morale was the lowest in the country" plus, and most significantly, the Force was said to have a "limited understanding" of the demand for its services. I felt totally exonerated by that last comment because the Force had ignored the public from the very start of the campaign to improve performance.

All that had changed between 2009 and 2015 was the change of a Chief Constable and a swathing austerity campaign launched by the Tory party. Indeed, the Chief Constable who had launched the performance campaign was still there in 2013 and his Deputy, the 'Chinless Wonder' was still there until September 2015.

In June 2015 eleven thousand calls for service from the public were either 'lost' or 'abandoned' in the Force system. That is cavalier in the extreme because I have already indicated that many calls are not responded to or do not result in positive action.

So, can I point the finger at Chief Officers in my Force? Well, yes, I can. They copied those Forces who had learned how to cheat with impunity. In doing that they gained a period of respite but allowed the deep organizational malaise of failure to penetrate even deeper and that eventually caused a Chief I never met to lose her job.

Chief Officers across England and Wales have a lot to answer for. Collectively they seem to have lost the ability to challenge the Government of the day. They are no longer players on the national stage as they have largely become robotic, grey men who seek to please whoever is in power. However, compared to Chief Officers, politicians of all complexions are by far the greater evil in the cause of todays policing problems.

I return to the 1964 Commission report on the Police. That piece of work established what the Police were supposed to do, but since then crime has changed immensely. We have terrorism, cybercrime, sophisticated fraud, people trafficking, increased volumes of drug dealing and a whole host of new and more sophisticated crimes. So, do the police now do exactly what they have always done plus all the other things that have arrived on the scene? If that is the expectation, then either there must be a massive increase in police resources, or some new body must be created.

In 1978, the year I joined the Police Service, the subdivision I was attached to had over seventeen police officers patrolling the street at any one time. There were seven car beats and ten foot beats, plus there were a species called neighbourhoods which had their own officer. I am told that in October 2018, an area larger than my first subdivision deployed only three double crewed cars for a whole night shift. Since I retired, in 2008, there has been a twenty percent reduction in the number of officers attached to Neighbourhood Policing Teams.

The resources that the police must deploy to incidents such as the Manchester bombing are huge and the cost, in addition to the human tragedies, runs into millions of pounds. Clearly things cannot go on as they currently are. The current Tory Government has promised that more money will be spent on one or two of the new crime areas, yet when you look into that money you find it has to be taken from existing police budgets. Something must stop being done if the new issues are to be addressed, yet Government never explains that. Areas of service disappear, and the public are left wondering why. The police become the scapegoat for the failings in providing a safe society, and they are not the best led organization in the world, but Government is the real culprit.

Successive governments have hidden behind the image of a failing Police Service. They have either grossly inflated the extra money they have allocated by double or triple counting of the same funds, or they have just blatantly reduced funding to 'balance the books'. There has been no consistent ideology behind all these cuts and broken promises because no one knows anymore what the Police are supposed to deliver. That is why I stress that there must be a new Royal Commission to create a service for the twenty first century and that needs to be one that the public can identify with.

In all this mess none of us should forget those officers and support staff who actually provide the service that is still depended on. They are facing enormous workloads and incredible stress just to get by; their working conditions are deplorable, and the pay and benefits are less than they were in my day. You seldom hear the voice of the real officers, and it is time a Royal Commission did; otherwise, they will also be consistently sold short by their own senior officers and whichever group of politicians is currently in power.

So, in conclusion, I miss the day-to-day rush, push and jostle of policing. I miss being part of a team and trying to make a difference. I miss the sense of belonging to something, but it is no longer clear what police officers actually do belong to. Being stabbed in the back seems even more prevalent than in my day. Would I join again? For years I have said there was no way I would ever cross the threshold of a police station again and yet? Armed with the benefit of retrospect, having learned from a myriad of mistakes, yes, I would join again. I could make an even bigger difference or maybe be seen as an even bigger nuisance than I was before.

FINALE

Having left the Police Service, I still needed to work to keep up the mortgage payments for a little longer. I could have applied for something completely different, but I wasn't quite finished with the battle against crime and disorder. There had been immense changes in the working of Crime and Disorder Reduction Partnerships and teams were emerging that worked on the same areas as the Neighbourhood Policing Teams. Meetings were introduced whereby a local councillor chaired a gathering that allowed members of the public to raise their concerns.

A job was advertised to work on one of the teams, assisting the councillors with their meetings, providing information on the issues that were raised and ensuring that those matters which were prioritized got actioned. I applied, was successful and, in spite of having to battle with a limited grasp of computers, I thoroughly enjoyed it.

Within a short period of time the new system was up and running and, even in those early days, was able to point at some significant achievements. I enjoyed the interaction with the politicians, having to persuade police officers instead of ordering them and the job seemed almost made for me.

I was again frustrated by the police approach to partnership working. The meetings that I was working on mirrored those which were an established part of the Neighbourhood Policing Teams. Our meetings were attended by staff from the local police teams and their efforts were monitored as part of the CDRP whole. Then the Police decided that they would introduce a meeting to liaise with the public. They already had such a meeting, provided through people like myself working within the CDRP. However, the Police just have to have their own, so they created another one and expected all those at the first meeting to attend theirs. This was duplication gone mad. They launched their meeting under a banner called 'The Pledge' and they were granted an award by some central government office. The result was that two almost identical meetings were being run with the public no doubt totally perplexed as to which forum to attend to get some action.

I spent hours acting as an adviser to councillors about policing and community safety in general. However, I was once again becoming more than a little frustrated by the arrogance of senior police officers towards their partners. Then out of the blue I saw a job advertised that looked like it had been made for me. The post was that of adviser on partnerships to the Police Authority of my old Force. This was a chance to really get to the heart of partnership working in the Police.

I had almost missed the deadline, but I completed the application form and drove it some forty miles to deliver it personally. Now it was my turn to show a little arrogance. I assumed that I would get an interview and so I rang the Police Authority offices to find out when the interviews would be. To my complete surprise the selection process had been completed. I was staggered, how could I not at least have received an interview. I had been the Forces' Partnership Manager; I had been a director of the Community Safety Network which developed the training programme for those working in community safety partnerships and I had been offered the role of Partnership and Neighbourhood Policing Officer in Government Office. Who could have been better qualified?

For a couple of days, I was existing in a vacuum. I could think of nothing but the implied rejection in denying me an interview. Then I received a phone call which purported to offer me feedback about my application. I was told that my experience had not been recent enough and there were some really excellent candidates. To this day I cannot understand the brass neck of the person trying to persuade me that I had been excluded legitimately.

Firstly, I was still working in partnerships and had had only a break of one month after leaving the Police Force. Secondly, an office junior had been given an interview! Well, let's be honest, that candidate was not the office junior, she was the most junior person in the Police Authority, but she was a graduate and a very competent person. Thirdly, none of the really excellent external candidates were successful. Fourthly, the job went to a friend of the Chief Executive of the Police Authority who had once been a member of the CID Mafia.

Was I bitter? Yes, I bloody was, I was incandescent. I am certain I would have won an equal opportunity case against the Police Authority. It would have been a real battle, as all those involved would have closed ranks in solidarity, but I do still believe in justice. However, I did not pursue the legal course because, after much soul searching, I did not think I could have been happy working with people as dishonest as those on the selection panel. Further, the atmosphere at work must have resembled that of a cess pit. I left my job with the Crime and Reduction Partnership, sold our house and moved lock, stock and barrel to Cyprus.

I have spent less time on the beach than I would have anticipated but on several of my visits there I have put old enmities to the back of my mind. After all, in the Police and the Police Authority there are the good, the bad and the dodgy, just as I have found in life. Does God pay back the bad? Well, the Police Authority no longer exists; throughout England and Wales those bodies were removed as being ineffectual. The Force continued to be branded a failure and, by implication, so have been the careers of many of the Chief Officers involved. Maybe the only person who has done really well in all this is the businessman involved in the episode with which I began this story. He continues to flourish, a wealthy entrepreneur and a pillar of society. Maybe I followed the wrong profession after all.

Thank you for reading. I hope it has brought you some enjoyment. It has certainly helped me lay a few ghosts.

GLOSSARY OF TERMS

Policing Styles.

There is a huge volume of research work on the styles of policing that are employed in the United Kingdom. Most police officers will not consider the style that they are adopting from day to day but in broad terms there are three major styles. These are,

'Watchman'. Here officers are maintaining order through informal measures with little thought about proactive prevention. Basically they are performing the medieval function of 'watch and ward' where gates are guarded and their very presence can be seen as a deterrent.

'Legalistic'. This style focuses on violations of the law and relies on threats of arrest or actual arrest. Here there is strict enforcement of the law. New Labour seemed to believe that they could carry out social engineering by creating new laws that the police would enforce rigidly. However, like all styles this is only part of the whole.

'Service'. This style sees elements of the other styles but the emphasis is on providing a service to the community or individual citizens. Here the provision of a service ensures that there is a real focus on solving the problems that people are facing using all the tools available to the police and other agencies.

(For further information on styles I suggest reference to: John Randolph Fuller, 'Criminal Justice, mainstream and crosscurrents.' Oxford University Press.

LOCAL POLICING TEAMS:

LPT's were first discussed in my Force early in 2001. The idea was the 'brain child' of our then Chief Constable. The intention was to increase the number of uniform police officers on the streets. The Crime Investigation Department (CID) and the Traffic Department were broken up and the officers who had worked there were distributed across the new LPT's. Thirty nine LPT's were created an sixteen million pounds were spent on refurbishing or building new police bases. LPT's never really worked, there were times when there were no specialisms available crime rose and the motorways were often left without police cover. Also in the first months there was no one to open the new bases and the public found it difficult access police services. It was a good idea and in many ways a precursor of the Neighbourhood Policing Teams, but there had been a failure to plan prior to their introduction and in consequence they had no chance of success.

NEIGHBOURHOOD POLICING TEAMS:

NPT's are a different concept from LPT's and were a Government initiative from the outset. The idea was to have a team in place for every community by 2008. The teams were to cover an area of about four square miles in urban areas and ten square miles in more rural areas. Each team is made up of ten to fifteen police officers under the command of a sergeant or inspector. There are around 3,600 teams covering England and Wales. These teams also incorporate Police Community Support Officers (PCSO'S), wardens, volunteers and other council staff. They aim to find real solutions to concerns raised by communities using a Problem Solving Model.

PROBLEM SOLVING POLICING:

This is by no means a new concept. It was originated by an American professor, Herman Goldstein, and involves the identification and analysis of crime or disorder problems so that an effective response strategy can be developed. The problem solving policing model was developed to replace the old reactive, incident driven style of policing that resulted in a work force chasing demand.

The essence of PSP is to obtain all available information, formulate a plan of action, take the action and feed the results back to the community. If done properly the team/Force will end up with a library of tried tested and proven responses.

CRIME AND DISORDER ACT 1998:

A piece of landmarked legislation introduced by the first Blair Government. Local Authorities were given more responsibility for developing strategies to reduce crime and disorder. The Act introduced Crime and Disorder Reduction Partnerships; introduced Anti Social Behaviour Orders, Parenting Orders, Sex Offender Orders and focused on 'racially aggravated offences.'

CRIME AND DISORDER PARTNERSHIPS:

CDRPs' were introduced by the 1998 Act and brought together the Police, probation service, local authorities, health authorities, social landlords, the voluntary sector, local residents, businesses and virtually everyone else who had an interest or stake in reducing the incidence of crime or disorder. Meetings took place at a strategic level but they also played a tasking role on local delivery teams.

ASSOCIATION OF CHIEF POLICE OFFICERS:

For many years ACPO was a not for profit, private, limited company. Its' purpose was primarily to lead to the development of policing practices in England and Wales and Northern Ireland. Established in 1948 ACPO provided a forum for the discussion of ideas and the coordination of strategic and operational responses to policing issues. The organization had a number of business areas such as terrorism and these provided best practice, guidance and policy.

ACPO was not, as it was often thought to be, a staff association in the same way that the Police Federation was for junior ranks. The staff association for Chief Police Officers is CPOSA (The Chief Police Officers Staff Association.

On the first of August 2015 ACPO was replaced by a new organization, namely, the National Police Chiefs' Council.

THE POLICE FEDERATION:

The Police Federation of England and Wales is the statutory staff association for constables, sergeants, inspector and chief inspector ranks. Police officers are not allowed to be members of trade unions or to take industrial action and in consequence the PFE&W play an important role for the 120,000 or so police officers in England and Wales.

THE SUPERINTENDENTS ASSOCIATION:

This body performs a very similar role to CPOSA and the PFE&W for the 1,600 or thereabouts superintending ranks in England and Wales.

Neighbourhood Watch:

Neighbourhood Watch is effectively a partnership which brings people together to make communities safer. Neighbourhood watches vary in size with one or more individuals performing a coordinating role. The coordinators collect membership fees and disseminate information leaflets, security advice etc. Often the watches are grouped together into areas and have professional coordinators at group level. My Force had a paid coordinator in each CDRP area and the Force had a central Chief Executive to whom the coordinators reported. This centralized management with volunteers working for their areas the Neighbrhood Watch became a significant representative of the voluntary sector and were used regularly when the Police were bidding for Government money. Our Neighborhood Watch were responsible for securing and training volunteers for many police roles such as staffing the public desks at Neighbourhood Policing bases.

Printed in Great Britain
by Amazon